W9-DFW-437

OIL PAINTING *for Everyone*

BY THE SAME AUTHOR

PRACTICAL PORTRAIT PAINTING

OIL PAINTING
for Everyone

by FRANK SLATER

NEW YORK
CHARLES SCRIBNER'S SONS

A-10.58[H]

THIS BOOK PUBLISHED SIMULTANEOUSLY IN
THE UNITED STATES OF AMERICA AND IN CANADA—
COPYRIGHT UNDER THE BERNE CONVENTION

Text PRINTED IN THE UNITED STATES OF AMERICA
Illustrations PRINTED IN HOLLAND
Library of Congress Catalog Card Number 58-10860

CONTENTS

OIL PAINTING *for Everyone*

1 An Approach to Painting in Oils

Before a teacher can begin to help a student, it is essential that they get to know one another. Teaching is based on the power to communicate. The instructor must be sure that everything he says, every phrase he uses is perfectly clear to the pupil. I propose to define the exact meaning of all technical terms so that the student, not yet familiar with the craft of oil painting will not be confused in any way. I should like to feel that anyone wishing to learn the first steps in oil painting will find this book useful, whether he is a mature adult who has never held a brush, or a young student just starting on a career.

Today, more and more older people are painting for "fun." Is painting "fun"? Strictly speaking, no. To paint well is one of the deepest satisfactions that exists. It can give lasting pleasure. Mature people who follow the principles in this book may find that "fun" ceases and true enjoyment begins. If you decide to take up painting and are prepared to work hard, this book will prove helpful. I have taught many older people who found this form of creative work brought them a new awareness of the world around and a deeper meaning to their lives.

Some "Sunday painters" prefer to paint what they like without the "drudgery" of learning to draw or paint with technical skill. The results vary from terrible to original and amusing. Your work usually reflects your personality, but in painting, lack of technical skill may get in the way of self-expression. A good technique helps you to express your thoughts and ideas freely and to overcome the inherent difficulties of the medium which arise between you and what you wish to say.

One amusing and courageous elderly woman of my acquaintance has been painting for many years without more than elementary knowledge of "good" painting. It has been a source of endless pleasure to her. When I see her numerous canvases covered at random with flowers and fruit, seascapes and animals, I am left without suitable comment. Should her work be considered seriously? Has it any inherent value? I hesitate to make a final judgment. Exceptional talent and a fresh approach have sometimes overcome lack of technical training, as in the cases of Grandma Moses and Henri Rousseau. Who is the final arbiter of talent? All experienced artists, art critics, connoisseurs and art historians consider their opinions of value; yet who have disagreed more among themselves than experts in art? The history of painting is full of their bitter quarrels, and experts have again and again been proved wrong by the passage of time. The Impressionists caused an uproar in Paris in the '70's and '80's, and the Post-Impressionists caused an uproar in London in 1910. Picasso is still a controversial figure. Jacob Epstein the sculptor, once reviled by the champions of traditional art, is now looked on as old-fashioned by the new school of wire and concrete. Today there is a trend towards complete freedom of expression, unfettered by technique and uninhibited by tradition. The Sunday painter paints for his own amusement. If he thinks that his pleasure would be spoiled by too careful study, by all means let him give full rein to his feelings. I am trying to be of help to those who wish to make use of a simple technique to guide them on their way. Lady Bracknell said, in *The Importance of Being Earnest,* "Ignorance is like a delicate, exotic fruit; touch it and the bloom is gone." There is a great deal of truth in this, and perhaps some amateurs are best advised to remain untutored and let their imagination range freely. Those who are interested in representational painting will do best to acquire technical knowledge, otherwise they are bound to feel frustrated and the inherent difficulties of painting will hinder their development.

President Eisenhower and Sir Winston Churchill are serious Sunday painters who have had the advantage of expert professional advice. Both busy men, with enormous loads of responsibility, they have turned to painting as a welcome escape into another form of concentrated work. They found it gave a feeling of relaxation, by taking them, for the time being, into a completely different world. Neither plays at painting. Sir Winston is now able to spend many weeks at a time at his easel, and his work is of an excellent professional standard. The President paints a good portrait, which

Sir Winston does not seem to have attempted, and obviously gets a good likeness with, I should imagine, the aid of photographs. Both men have demonstrated the value of painting for relaxation and enjoyment only, not by messing about, but by taking the hobby seriously and really working at it, however hard their own jobs may have been. When it comes to painting, "if a thing is worth doing, it's worth doing well," was never more true.

How are you to know if you have genuine talent or not? Talent is revealed by an irresistible urge to express itself. You will constantly be drawing or painting for the sheer love of it. You will also undoubtedly show some facility. If you are young, the problem that may face you is whether your talent is sufficiently important on which to build a career and become the central focus of your life. If there is clear evidence of some talent, combined with a strong creative urge, it is essential to study seriously for a while to see how it will develop. A true talent given a chance to grow in favorable circumstances will soon show unmistakable signs of its quality. The opinion of a qualified professional artist is of great value. If favorable, it can give encouragement, or if unfavorable, may even stimulate you to greater effort. There is no substitute for talent and without it, all the hard work and conscientious endeavor will be of no avail. Should it soon become apparent that talent is nonexistent, or too small to be of value, the time spent studying will not have been entirely wasted. It will have been a good thing to have gained a knowledge of the difficulties of painting and the limitations of your abilities.

Up to the age of fourteen or fifteen, most children have an ability to express themselves in color. At school they are rightly encouraged to paint freely and happily, giving full reign to their imagination. Children are usually uninhibited in their work without any knowledge of form, perspective or proportion. The results are often gay and colorful, but never of any real artistic value. Somewhere in early adolescence this freedom of expression disappears. The young person becomes self-conscious, aware of his limitations, involved in other forms of activity, and loses both his interest and his powers. All except those with talent.

Talent is a rare and precious gift. It is the duty of all who possess it to cultivate and develop it to its fullest extent. It is the duty of parents of young people with talent to see that this is possible. To crush or waste it is a crime against life itself.

Now I have made it clear that I am talking to the young man or woman with unmistakable talent, or the older person who believes he or she can get real satisfaction from painting and wishes to work hard to acquire the foundation of his craft. I have specifically used the word "craft." Oil painting is a craft. It CAN be learned.

What exactly does painting consist of? Before we go any further, it is necessary to answer this seemingly simple question. For our immediate purpose, I am dealing entirely in representational painting in oils.

Painting consists of creating a true image of the objects we are attempting to represent. The objects have two major aspects which we have to understand and record—color and form. Not only must we fully grasp their color and form, but also their relationship to each other, and to their surroundings. Painting, besides being a craft which can be learned, is also an emotional activity involving personal interpretation. For the moment I'm defining only the "craft."

What does the word color mean? A lemon is yellow, a cherry red, a leaf green. When a child attempts to indicate these facts, he dips his brush in yellow, red, or green paint and fills in the outline of the subject already drawn. This fulfills his need to express color. The result is completely flat and the color is no more than "coloring." It is a formal symbol of the object. In reality, a lemon as we observe it is only a true "lemony" color on a small area of its surface, the tone of yellow becoming deeper as it recedes from the light, and quite dark in the shadow. "Coloring" or "local color" is the red of the rose, the green of the tree, the blue of the sky. "Color" is the relationship or harmony between one color and another either in the same object or between one object and another. It is by learning to see these color *relationships* correctly and matching them truly, one against the other, that we achieve the illusion of reality.

What is form? The form of an object is its solid shape. It is an entirely separate idea from its color. Where color changes with the passing shadow or time of day, the form is permanent.

I hesitate to define the word art. It has been defined a thousand times, each time with a different emphasis according to the point of view of the writer or artist. One thing most people are agreed on—it is impossible to teach anyone how to become an artist. A student can be guided, taught how to develop his personal gifts, and exposed to the work of the best artists, but whatever makes him a true artist must come from within. I believe that much time and effort can be saved in the development of an artist if he acquires a good foundation of craftsmanship and a mastery over his paint to make it express what he wishes. All good painters have something to say that can be expressed in terms of color and form. They may not at first be certain what it is they want to express, only that paint is the medium they want to use.

There has never been a more confusing time for the artist than today. Standards of painting that lasted with few changes for centuries seem to have been cast aside in the last fifty years. After the Impressionist movement began with Manet and Pissarro in the middle of the last century, traditional barriers were broken down by artists like Monet and Renoir, followed by Van Gogh and Gauguin. New frontiers were extended by Cezanne and fresh horizons revealed by Picasso. Nevertheless, good painting remains good painting in spite of all revolutions, even if it is sometimes difficult to recognize at the time. It has never been easy to judge original contemporary work. There will always be the rebel of genius who will upset prevailing standards. This book is not addressed to original genius, which in any event goes its own way and is extremely rare. I believe your eye and mind can be trained effectively to *see* and to be able to put down your interpretation of what you see. A solid foundation of good craftsmanship is essential.

I am not one who thinks it is necessary to study drawing for years before attempting to paint in oils. I think it perfectly feasible to learn both crafts at the same time. The best way to learn oil painting is to start by painting still life, and the best way to learn drawing is to work from life, when possible from the nude model. It is a good thing to carry a sketchbook and to draw whatever interests you in the world around. The way to learn to draw is to draw, draw, draw. By constantly working, you will learn from your own mistakes and build up knowledge from experience. With a pencil and sketchbook you can study continuously. Draw your friends, your city, your countryside; draw men at work, or children at play; draw everything that catches your interest. A sound knowledge of drawing is bound up with good painting. I believe they can be studied side by side.

It is not necessary to learn to paint in water colors before attempting oils. The techniques are so different that it may even prove a handicap. In water color the paint, freely mixed with water, is brushed on in transparent washes, so that the white paper shows through. To make the tones lighter, you mix your paint with more water. In oil painting, the pigment is mostly opaque, and to make it lighter you mix it with more white, and not by thinning it with oil or turpentine, except under special circumstances. After starting with water color, the beginner in oils is apt to make his pigment too thin and use his thinner or "medium" as freely as he did water.

I made my own studies at the Royal Academy Schools in London where, besides having a permanent principal, a Royal Academician came as visiting instructor each month. This provided an excellent variety of outlook and showed there were many approaches to painting. One man stood out above all others, the great artist, Walter Sickert. He had studied under Whistler and Degas, and made it clear that we were lucky indeed to be able to receive knowledge handed down so directly in the great tradition. He pointed out that it was our duty to acquire what knowledge he had to give.

Much of this knowledge I am fortunate to have retained and shall pass on here. I have found it of inestimable value all my life. What you do with this knowledge when you have it is your affair. You may wish to paint in a completely non-objective manner, or in a traditional and representational one. The training which I suggest will help you to master the medium and find yourself. Each of us has something personal to say. We should not concern ourselves too much about its importance. That is for time to judge. If we have talent, our job is to get on with our work.

The young are naturally concerned about making a living. In a flourishing economy there is always room for the talented artist who knows his craft. Even if you do not succeed in becoming a completely independent artist, you may fit into one of the many jobs in the commercial field of illustration and advertising. You will certainly be able to make a living. If your chief aim is to make big money, then the profession of art is not for you. A few hit the jackpot, but the remainder must gain satisfaction in the deep joy of creative work. No one with talent should deny himself the opportunity to develop, and parents should do everything in their power to help and encourage. Drawing and painting should be studied on a full-time basis, five days a week at a good art school for two or three years at least. Less than this is barely sufficient. The artist, the writer, the musician, in fact, all free-lance professionals must have faith in their own ability and be prepared to take the risks of economic insecurity that are entailed. It is not an easy life, but the satisfaction it brings, makes it more than worthwhile.

Self-discipline is essential. You must learn to drive yourself hard. Talent divorced from character seldom gets very far.

My experience with small groups of students, whether young or not so young, has taught me a great deal about their characteristics. All beginners have much in common. They seldom realize what intense concentration is needed to paint well. A painter can be compared with a juggler. At first he learns to keep two or three oranges in the air, then finally six or more. This needs patience, practice, skill and above all, concentration. A painter has to make continuous judgments about color, tone, form relationships, edges and many other important problems simultaneously. It is chiefly the mind that must be skillful and the metaphor of the juggler is misleading if it makes painting seem a physical performance. Certainly a steady hand is necessary, and should obey the eye instantly, but the actual physical skill needed is elementary.

You may be in doubt what direction your work will take. How are you to find out? One simple rule is to paint what you love. Constable, the great English landscape painter, was happiest painting the Suffolk countryside he knew so well; Canaletto painted Venice; Cezanne, Provence; Renoir loved to paint women, children and flowers; Van Gogh only reached his full stature when he went to Arles where he fell in love with the sunlight. Portrait painters are endlessly interested in people. The essence of "modern" painting is the love of picture-making as an end in itself, form, color, and line balanced rhythmically to make a good picture. Whatever direction you choose, be sure it is based on an urgent need to interpret something you find exciting.

The essence of a picture is the emotion that sparked it to life in the first place. Whenever you look at a good picture, you should be able to feel the excitement that the artist experienced when he first conceived it.

Actually there is little choice in the matter of becoming an artist. You are driven to it whether you feel it wise or not. A true talent will overcome parental objection or financial difficulties and, combined with hard work, will bring success.

The older person, with an urge to take up painting for the first time, will find it an adventure of discovery that is bound to prove worthwhile.

2 Materials

Now let us consider the basic equipment necessary to start painting in oils, as well as some of the conditions under which you must work.

I fully realize the need for economy, especially for young people, but false economy is to be deplored and in the long run will prove wasteful and extravagant. It is impossible to do good work with inferior materials. Cheap canvas, an unsteady easel and crude colors will bring poor results. They make unnecessary difficulties, besides wasting precious time. Always get the best materials—it pays in the end.

EASEL

Let us begin with the easel. It must be strong and steady. If you cannot possibly afford a standard one, which costs about thirty dollars and will last a lifetime, then the best kind is the simple three-legged wooden type. If you use this kind be sure that your canvas is held firmly in place, either by a tilter (a device that clips to the easel as well as the top of your canvas, holding it vertical) or by an ordinary nail to hold it steady. As painting should often be a vigorous exercise, an unsteady easel will be a constant irritation. A good easel should allow the canvas to be moved freely up and down and should hold it in a vertical position, or even slightly tilted forward to avoid reflection from the source of light. So invest in a solid easel, a purchase which you will never regret.

PALETTE

A palette should be oval, about 24 inches across, and properly balanced. This is essential. Your hand supports it at a point away from the center of gravity, so unless it is weighted on the one side, your wrist will soon become painful, and it will be impossible to carry on. A correctly balanced oval palette is not expensive and will last forever.

BRUSHES

To begin with, you need a fair selection of good hog's hair brushes and one sable one. These can be added to gradually, two or three at a time as you progress, till you have a wide variety. Twelve would be the minimum number to begin with, ranging from fairly small, numbers 2 and 3, to large, numbers 11 and 12. I recommend brushes called *filberts*. They are slightly rounded at the top, shaped rather like a fingernail. I use them myself and find them ideal. Your sable brush, used only occasionally for delicate touches, should be round at the base, pointed at the top and fairly small, number 4 or number 5.

The brushes should be of the best quality and meticulously cleaned after each day's work. After wiping them free of thick paint, wash them in soap and hot water, and be sure that they are left in their original shape without hairs twisted in different directions. Dirty brushes harden in a few hours, lose their elasticity and become useless.

PAINTS

The basic colors required for working indoors are

Flake white	Viridian	Burnt Sienna
Cadmium red	Venetian red	Ivory black
Alizarin crimson	Cobalt	Cadmium yellow
Yellow ochre	French Ultramarine	

For landscape you will need a few more blues, greens and yellows which I shall mention in due course. Get a good standard make of "artist's," not "student's" oil paints. Use only the best quality. The order I have mentioned is the one in which I place the paints on the palette from right to left. The tubes can be obtained in what is known as "studio" size, but you will need a ½ lb. or 1 lb. tube of flake white, as this is used far more than any other pigment.

THINNER OR "MEDIUM"

You need a bottle of refined turpentine, a bottle of copal oil medium, which is fast drying, and a bottle of linseed oil, which is slower. A metal container is required to hold your medium and clips on to the top right hand corner of the palette.

PALETTE KNIFE

This is required to remove paint from the palette at the end of each session. After you have taken off most of the solid paint, the remainder can be wiped off with a rag and turpentine. I always wipe my palette completely clean after each day's work. You may also use the knife to remove paint from your canvas if you are dissatisfied with what you have done.

As you gain knowledge in handling oil paint, you may want to experiment with different methods of applying the pigment. Sometimes artists use a palette knife for this purpose instead of a brush. This technique is for the experienced only.

CHARCOAL

For drawing on canvas you need a fairly hard Venetian charcoal, sharpened to a point with a razor blade. A "putty" or kneaded rubber is used to remove charcoal completely.

CHARCOAL FIXATIVE AND SPRAY

Fixative is a preparation composed of varnish and spirit, which is sprayed on to the charcoal to keep it from rubbing off. After spraying, the spirit evaporates, leaving the drawing protected by the varnish.

RAGS

You need a full supply of cotton rags with which to clean your palette and for wiping your brushes.

CANVAS

This should be made of linen, and not cotton. It should have a good "tooth" or grain—not too rough, not too smooth. Useful sizes are 12 x 16, 14 x 18, 16 x 20, 20 x 24, 25 x 30. Do not try to save money by getting cheap, inferior canvas. Your paint will slip about, and you will soon lose control of it. A good quality canvas is essential. It should be lightly primed, priming being the preparation with which it is covered to prevent absorption through the pores of the canvas. All good artists' material shops sell primed canvas already stretched. It is not necessary to do this yourself, and I advise against it unless you are particularly skillful at that kind of job. A poorly stretched canvas is a great disadvantage. See that the pegs in the back are firmly hammered in to keep the canvas tightly stretched.

VARNISH AND RETOUCHING VARNISH

After you have painted over your work once or more, the darker portions sometimes "sink" a little into the canvas, look "dead" and drop in tone value. To restore them to their original strength you can use retouching varnish, a preparation specially prepared for this purpose. It is a mixture of resin and turpentine, and when applied at the beginning of a day's work makes the surface receptive as well as restoring the original values. It can also be applied when the painting is finished and will keep it looking fresh until it is ready for a permanent varnish. A picture should not be varnished with *mastic* varnish until it has been completed for at least six months. The reason for this is that although the paint may be dry to the touch, it is not yet chemically dry and will continue to contract for that length of time, causing cracking if varnish is applied too soon.

STUDIO CONDITIONS

Now for the best conditions under which to paint. You need light and space—these are absolutely essential. Light by which to see your subject clearly as well as the canvas, space to walk back to see your work at a distance. It is also important to paint in a room with a window of some height, so that the light falls on your subject over your left shoulder. This prevents your shadow from being cast either on the canvas or on what you are painting.

Choose a room with a north light, so that the sun never pours in to dazzle and constantly change the strength and direction of light. Try to avoid painting by artificial light, as it usually makes hard shadows and distorts the true color of the subject as well as your paints. If circumstances make it absolutely necessary to work at night, be sure that the light is completely masked from your eyes and is bright enough to show everything clearly. There are good "daylight" neon tubes which give a fair imitation of true daylight, and these are probably the most satisfactory to use.

Before we begin to use oil paint, we must know something of its physical nature, how it performs and reacts under our treatment, and the manner in which it should be handled.

Pigments are derived from many different sources, animal, vegetable, and mineral. It is not my purpose here to go into an analysis of their origin. Color-makers grind down the pigment to a powder and then mix the powder either with water or oil to make water colors or oil paints.

The use of oil paint and water colors differs widely. Water evaporates, but oil remains and hardens on contact with the atmosphere as a chemical process. While the paint is wet, you can paint freely *into* it, merging one brush stroke with another. Once it is dry, it cannot be made moist again, and must be repainted on top. This makes it imperative that you be satisfied with each day's work as far as it goes, before you leave it to dry.

Flake white mixed with other colors makes the paint thicker and richer, as well as paler and more opaque. In what is known as the "direct" method, light colors are made by mixing white with one or more other colors and not by thinning the color with oil and turpentine and letting the canvas shine through as does the white paper in water color.

There are exceptions to this, and some artists including Renoir, Cezanne and Matisse have sometimes used transparent "glazes" of color, thinned by oil and turpentine, over white canvas.

The "indirect" method separates the problems of form and color to begin with. You start by painting a foundation in monochrome, making a study of the forms and tone relationships in a light key, and then glazing the color on top with transparent or semi-transparent washes. At present I will discuss the "direct" method only, that is to say applying color straight on to the white canvas.

Oil paint can be opaque, semi-transparent or transparent, according to your needs. The more white paint you use with your color, the more opaque it will become, the more medium you mix with it, the more transparent.

Here are some of the characteristics of the paints and thinners you will be using.

CADMIUM RED A clear, bright red, useful at all times.

ALIZARIN CRIMSON Should be used sparingly as it tends to dominate. Useful for making purple, when mixed with blue.

YELLOW OCHRE Useful at all times.

VIRIDIAN A lovely strong green, useful at all times and never overpowering.

VENETIAN RED A good strong reddish-brown. Tends to be overpowering, but mixes well with viridian.

COBALT BLUE A useful and excellent color at all times.

FRENCH ULTRAMARINE A deep blue, useful color at all times.

BURNT SIENNA A strong brown, to be used sparingly except in rich warm darks.

IVORY BLACK A useful paint except where brightness is required.

CADMIUM YELLOW A strong, bright yellow, to be used sparingly indoors, but invaluable in effects of sunlight or when mixed with blue to make vivid greens.

LEMON YELLOW There is no substitute for this when a clear pale yellow is required.

TURPENTINE This thins the paint without making it more oily.

LINSEED OIL This makes the paint more malleable, but also more oily. If used too freely, it will make your paint slip and slide.

COPAL OIL MEDIUM This also makes the paint more malleable, but if used too freely, tends to become sticky, as it is a quick drier. If I want the paint to dry overnight, I use a mixture of turpentine and copal oil medium.

Most students are inclined to use too much medium. As a general rule it is best to use as little medium as possible, just enough to keep the paint malleable. You should thin your paint chiefly by mixing it into a paste on your palette. When you wish to cover a wide area rapidly, such as the background, by all means thin your paint with a mixture of oil and turpentine. Rubbing on paint forcefully with a brush to get rid of the white canvas is usually referred to as "scrubbing" it on.

During the first day's work, when you wish to cover the white canvas as soon as possible, a certain amount of medium is helpful. The moment you use too much the paint becomes runny and the surface slippery so that you cannot control your brush stroke. Only experience can tell you *exactly* how much to use, but always make it less than more.

I usually pour some turpentine into the small container attached to the palette and add a very little copal oil medium and a few drops of linseed oil. This mixture gives me just about the consistency I need.

A standard paint box is a useful piece of equipment to hold your materials, especially when traveling or working out-of-doors. If economy is necessary, it is wiser to spend your money on good quality paints and brushes than on an elaborate paint box.

3 A Word on Drawing

Painting is concerned with color and form, drawing with form only. You can draw in pencil, chalk, charcoal or with a brush, but whatever medium you use you should be concerned chiefly with the shapes of things and their relations to one another.

Drawing is an intellectual exercise that needs the greatest concentration. If I see a pencil sketch executed in a few minutes, I can make a fair estimate of the artist's intellectual gifts. Although feeling can be delicately or forcefully expressed in a drawing, good draughtsmanship is largely the result of keen intellectual qualities.

Drawings can be divided into two categories: those done as a preparation for a larger work, and those carried out as an end in themselves. As this book is about painting, I shall deal mainly with the first category.

There are few more interesting aspects of an artist's work than the preparatory sketches he makes for a painting. The drawings of Michelangelo and Da Vinci, Rembrandt and Rubens, Ingres and Degas and other supreme draughtsmen can be studied with the greatest pleasure for their sensitivity to form and power of observation, quite apart from their intrinsic beauty. In a drawing, no richness of paint or color can cover up inadequacies of form. It brings us into the closest contact with the artist's mind and reveals his immediate reactions to nature.

I have heard beginners say that they don't care to work with the point of a pencil. I have also heard recruits say that they don't care for drilling on the barracks square. How else can they expect to become good soldiers?

Drawing can be fun as well as hard work. If you carry a sketch book around with you it can become a valuable record of your visual experiences and many of the drawings could be used for future paintings.

The best way to learn to draw is from a live model, clothed or nude. The purpose of studying from the nude is to gain knowledge, not only of the subtle changes of form, one flowing rhythmically into the other, but of the structure of the body itself. A working knowledge of anatomy is useful but need not be exhaustive.

In my student days, art schools taught you first to draw from the "antique," the classical Greek and Roman statues of antiquity. The danger of this was that you were liable to copy the complex forms without understanding their intrinsic structure. After you had progressed to the Life Class, and learned something of the human body in action, you returned to the antique with a new understanding of how to recreate the cold plaster casts in their true formal beauty.

The purpose of drawing is to recreate on a flat surface the three-dimensional qualities of the object or scene before you, selecting only those visual aspects that are needed to reveal the forms. As soon as drawing is concerned with tonal qualities, as in a full-toned charcoal drawing, it crosses into the sphere of painting. One simple test of a good drawing is that a sculptor could work from it. If a sound craftsman is drawing unself-consciously, the result will have a beauty of its own. To illustrate my point I have used working drawings by Rembrandt and Degas. The portrait by Ingres is an example of a drawing done as an end in itself. I do not propose here to deal with problems of anatomy, perspective and other specialized subjects.

> If you wish to train yourself to draw well, begin by placing a few simple objects together and draw them in pencil on cartridge paper pinned firmly to a drawing board. You should work sitting down and prop your board on the back of a chair to keep it steady. Take a "B" pencil, with a long, sharp point, and make a sketch of the group as described on pages 33 and 34. I can see no purpose in making more than a working drawing. Do not carry it too far, as this is purely an exercise. Pencil has its own beauty as a medium and by varying the pressure you can make your line softer or harder to express the form.

A good drawing is made up of Line and Modeling and *not* Outline and Shading. The word "outline" suggests a hard inexpressive boundary as used in a map. Line is a living, expressive means of revealing form. Artists like Picasso and Rodin have been able to suggest complete solidity by line alone.

"Shading" implies meaningless tones to represent shadows. The way modeling is suggested must depend on the convention used by the artist. Leonardo Da Vinci used a technique which has become a classic of diagonal lines both slanting across and round the form. As the natural movement of the wrist is diagonally north-east, south-west, it is certainly a convenient one.

Besides modelling round the forms you have to be aware of the cast shadows made by solid objects and treat them differently from the modelling. They should be lightly suggested. When they fall on nearby objects they help to reveal the forms on which they are cast. The crispness with which a pencil can be used enables you to make darker accents when necessary but no attempt at tone relationships should be made. You are using a convention and not making a photographic copy.

After making a few studies of still life, begin to make sketches of more complex subjects, either indoors or out. Get friends to pose for you and make studies of them in action and repose. Be self-critical and try to improve on your efforts each time. Avoid the use of indiarubber, except to erase completely. Your approach to a drawing should be one of a tentative statement, feeling for the truth very lightly but firmly and then, using your first attempt as a guide, follow it by a more definite and expressive line. From the first, think across the form, searching for anything that will reveal solidity. Most forms can be thought of as either basically eggs, cylinders, cubes and so on. A head is typically egg-shaped, arms and legs cylinders, furniture and houses cubes. A bare tree with its branches spreading out from the main trunk, makes an excellent subject for the study of solid forms in continually changing direction. Drawing with a pencil should stimulate you to select essentials and to put them down in their order of priority. Nothing should ever be vague or unresolved. Every touch should convey exactly what it is supposed to, however delicately and lightly drawn.

Conté and chalk pencil and many similar types of crayons are excellent for rapid and effective work when you have achieved some mastery with a pencil, although they smudge easily and hardly erase at all. If you use toned paper, white chalk can be used for indicating highlights, but be careful not to let your drawings deteriorate into a tone study. When you use a brush to draw your subject onto canvas, your touch should still be expressive, even though it is going to be covered soon afterwards. Every stroke you put on canvas contributes some effect to the final picture.

4 Fundamentals of Painting

The best way to learn the fundamentals of painting is to attempt a simple still life group consisting of three or more objects placed against a background. The study of these objects and their relation to each other and their surroundings, will bring out most of the basic problems of painting.

In life, nothing exists in a vacuum. The tree grows in the field and is seen against the sky or the hill. The vase stands on the table which is on the floor of a room and is seen with a wall behind it. If we put together a group of still life, we are really making a miniature of the way life looks around us, rather as a stage set in the theater is meant to represent life.

For a still life group, it is best to choose objects with different surfaces and textures, simple in color and form. A bottle or a vase may be shiny, a book may be matt. When we paint this group, we are re-creating their forms and colors on canvas so that we shall recognize at once the nature of each. If you look at a shiny bottle, it has a great many different color values. Some may be green, some gray and some almost white. Looking at this combination of values communicates to our senses that it is made of glass and not metal or china, which would create a different set of color values. If the value of the background is truly related to the value of the object in front, we sense the distance between them and the space around the object. When you begin to study, it is wise to keep as close to nature as possible. As you develop and gain confidence, your color may become more personal and express your individual vision.

When two or more colors are placed side by side, they have an effect on each other.

Let us take a light color and observe the effect when it is placed alongside other colors.

Mix a light green shade and place it next to a dark red patch, next to a light red one, and against one of exactly the same value in red as it is in green. Notice how the green, which is the same color each time, takes on a different aspect. We shall soon see when we begin to paint, that no one color exists by itself, but is affected by the colors immediately surrounding it. A light color looks lighter when placed beside a dark one, and in turn, the dark one seems darker. If the green is placed next to white, it actually loses much of its brightness, whereas against black it appears most brilliant of all.

One of the errors of judgment which you will often make is caused by this optical illusion. You are constantly being tempted to make darks darker and lights lighter, especially when light and dark values are in juxtaposition.

When painting, I stand a certain distance away from the easel—about two or three feet—my right foot well in front of my left. I start by holding four or five brushes in my left hand, which is also holding the palette and a clean rag. I take one brush in my right hand to mix my first color, and as soon as I have painted it on to the canvas, I take a second brush and mix the color to be placed alongside the first. I may use the first brush again to restate the value of the color more accurately and continue with these two until I mix a third color value. As the painting continues I may use as many as ten to twenty brushes, depending on the amount of ground to be covered, holding six or eight in my left hand and placing the others immediately available in a jar. I constantly wipe them on the rag to remove superfluous paint and when I find that they are getting clogged, I take the whole bunch, immerse them in some turpentine and wipe them clean. I keep as many as twenty or thirty clean brushes at hand and never hesitate to take another if I want to mix a completely fresh color.

Most beginners hold their brushes too low down when they are working, almost as if they were writing. This is a *very* bad habit and leads to tight and niggly work. You should hold your brush as high up the stem as you can manage. This allows you to paint freely and directly.

The actual physical action with which you mix colors on your palette is important. It should be vigorous and complete in performance, so that the two colors mixed together make a definite new color of their own.

I have heard many beginners mention the mixing of colors as if there were some mysterious trick involved. This is far from the case. Mixing is a straightforward process and, if done the right way, should present few difficulties.

Suppose you wish to mix a certain tone of green. Begin by taking some viridian, assuming it to be the paint nearest in color to what you require, and mix it with a little white, using your judgment as to the amount of each necessary. This will give you a particular color value of green to start with. Compare it with the part of the green object in front of you that you are immediately painting, and decide whether the green you require is either more blue or more yellow, darker or lighter than what is on your palette. According to your judgment you then add some cobalt or French ultramarine, yellow ochre or cadmium yellow, and, perhaps, more white. You mix them together vigorously until you have a definite, new color. When you are fairly certain that you have arrived at the true color, apply it firmly to the canvas and compare it to what you are painting. Should you still not be satisfied and feel it requires a little more exactness, it is not necessary to remove it, as you will find it useful as a guide. When you have finally mixed the right color, paint it forcefully *into* your first brush stroke and continue to use the right value with absolute conviction.

A beginner can be expected to do this perfectly well. Anybody who has had to match one color with another in daily life, whether it is socks and tie or bag and gloves, is used to making judgments of this kind.

The whole craft of oil painting is based on approaching the truth by stages. If your attempts are too wild, it is best to remove them completely with a rag, but even an experienced painter has to build up to his exact color relationships, seldom attempting to get their full strength immediately. A painting should develop organically, gradually growing to completion without drastic changes of plan. I have often heard it said that oil paint is easy to alter. This is far from the case. Naturally, every touch you make "alters" the look of the work and you have considerable freedom to make changes into wet paint. If you have made serious errors in drawing or composition during the first day's work, it is better to remove it entirely with a rag and turpentine than to continue on a poor foundation. If you should decide at some later stage to alter something radically because it is unsatisfactory, alterations should be made boldly, even first scraping off some of the underpainting with a palette knife, and then merging the new area into the surroundings with care. The more free the general handling, the more easily changes can be made. In the case of a portrait, alterations at a late stage can spoil the freshness and quality. Any painting that has been messed about by continual changing will look the poorer, however much you try to cover it up.

Careful planning should prevent the need for drastic alterations. You should have all the opportunity you require for experiment and minor changes when the paint is wet each day.

The process of painting from day to day is one of building up one surface on top of another. The effect of what lies beneath is very important, especially when your paint is transparent or semi-transparent, as in very dark areas. If, for instance, you are painting dark hair or black velvet, you should use a warm brown tone underneath which will glow through the cool black on top. If you paint black over black the result will look heavy and dull.

When mixing very dark colors you naturally use little or no white. At all other times the rich, creamy quality that is characteristic of oil paint, is achieved by mixing the colored pigment with white. Occasionally, when you want to obtain a particularly bright color, you will find there is a limit to the amount of white you can use without losing brilliance. Sometimes only the pure pigment itself will give you the required effect, either used thickly, or transparently over the white canvas. Do not get into the habit of using paint transparently, otherwise you will find yourself using oils as if they were water colors and relying on the white surface underneath instead of mixing with white paint to get your correct values.

The terms "warm" and "cool" need defining. Blue is the coldest color and red the warmest. When the light is cool, as from a window facing north, surfaces on which the light falls are affected, and are relatively cooler than those that are turned away. If the rhythm of warm and cool alternate across your canvas, it is not only a pleasing effect but gives a lifelike quality to the picture. All local coloring of the objects you are painting is affected by it, and if the surfaces are at all shiny and reflect light directly, as in the case of flesh, it is of the utmost importance to see the alternating harmony of warm and cold.

A common habit I have observed in beginners, is the one of pushing the paint about unnecessarily once it is on the canvas, expecting by this means to alter its color. If the color is wrong, pushing it around will never make it right. It is a bad thing to push, prod and fiddle the paint once it is on the canvas. Either restate it in the right color, or if it is too unsatisfactory, remove it altogether. Each time you mix a color and put in on canvas, you should be performing a definite action with a specific purpose in mind, prompted by a clear thought. This gives your painting "quality."

What is "quality" in oil painting? Quality is the beauty of texture and the rich surface that comes only as a result of using your oil paint with confidence and knowledge. If you niggle and fiddle, hesitate and dither, the surface becomes messy and unpleasant.

Good quality takes many forms, varying from the thick impasto of Rembrandt and Van Gogh to the rich, velvety surface of Vermeer, the variations of texture of Picasso or the smooth limpidity of Matisse. Monet built up a beautiful surface quality by placing one thickly painted brush stroke of pure rich color alongside, and sometimes over another. Toulouse-Lautrec employed a long downward stroke, with occasional cross-hatching, which gave his work a characteristic quality of its own.

The surface quality of an oil painting can be appreciated not only for its physical beauty, but for its aesthetic appeal. This derives partly from an awareness of the power of the artist over his material and his ability to use it with freedom and joy.

Sometimes, when watching students at work, I have suddenly turned to one and asked, "What exactly do you think you are doing now?" Usually they have been unable to answer. Of course, there are times when a painter is so carried away by his feelings that he could not explain in so many words what he is doing. I merely wish to emphasize that the way to learn the craft of painting is to consider it a process of judgments and decisions, dictated by a clear mind and carried out with logic and careful thinking. Your feelings will quite often govern your actions, but at no time should you be caught aimlessly fiddling. With experience you will paint more and more by instinct and intuition, and allow yourself to be carried along by your feelings. Just as a poet can write a sonnet filled with emotion and keep respect for its form, so you must learn to express yourself freely and yet keep a respect for your craft.

5 *How to Paint a Still Life*

I plan to complete our first attempt at still life in one long day's work or in two morning sessions. I should like to think that you are going to work along with me, and will yourselves compose a group similar to the one chosen here. I have, as you can see in the illustration, chosen a simple group: a green bowl, a slim blue book and a lemon. I have placed them on a red cloth, with a pale cream background.

Be sure that your group is almost at eye level, if necessary raising the table on which it is placed. The light should be coming over your left shoulder, and the easel placed about three or four feet from the group. There should be at least six feet clear behind you to walk back.

The objects are arranged so that they touch and cover portions of each other as things do in real life.

Our first operation is to draw the group on canvas so that it fits the space to the greatest advantage. For this purpose, I use a piece of charcoal.

The reason I choose charcoal is because it can be brushed off in a moment if my first attempt is not entirely satisfactory, leaving no marks behind as paint is liable to do. My intention is not to make a detailed preliminary drawing. "Operation Charcoal" is solely concerned with the placing of the objects within the four sides of the canvas. A painting should be carried out entirely with a brush. Your freedom of attack should not be restricted by a rigid drawing underneath. As insufficient planning can spoil the effect of otherwise good work, I allow myself the opportunity of seeing the composition on canvas before starting to paint. A matter of half an inch one way or the other can upset the balance, and it is not always easy to hit the right placing immediately on a blank canvas. I prefer to make a kind of relief map in charcoal and then, after fixing it lightly, brush most of it off, leaving the merest suggestion behind.

We are ready to begin. The piece of charcoal should be fairly hard, about four inches long and sharpened to a point by a razor blade.

Where are we to put our first touch? Why in one place rather than another? The answer is, as usual, based on logic. There must be room at the bottom of the canvas to show the objects firmly placed on the table. This will give stability to the composition. Start where one object touches another, and you will immediately begin by thinking in terms of relationships.

A good place to start is where the base of the bowl meets the lemon, thus placing the lemon and the bowl firmly in relation to each other and to the bottom of the canvas. Feel your way to the left side of the bowl and along the top of the lemon to the right side. Complete the form of the lemon. Draw each side of the bowl related to one another, judge where the horizontal edge of the foreground meets the background, complete the lid of the bowl. Now draw the firm, vertical side of the book, behind the bowl, the base of the book next to the lemon, then the other two vertical edges. See that the base of the background on one side relates correctly to the other. Finally draw the top of the book, in correct perspective.

As you carry out this exercise, be sure to show that these objects are solid. This is done by lightly indicating the modeling as you go along, as well as the cast shadows of the objects themselves. You are drawing three solid objects standing on the same flat surface, related to one another, which cannot be suggested by outline alone.

If you are satisfied that you have placed the group agreeably on the canvas, spray the drawing with a little charcoal fixative. After a few moments, take a clean rag and brush off any superfluous charcoal. You do not require the drawing as an accurate foundation for your painting. It is merely to give you the right starting place for your brush. If you are not entirely satisfied with the placing of your first attempt, do not hesitate to rub it off and try again.

Before you start to paint, be sure that your materials are conveniently placed for use. Painting is such concentrated work needing continuous, fluent thought, that you do not want it to be interrupted constantly by groping for brushes and unscrewing tubes of paint. Have your painting table close by your side, with the brushes upright in a jar, your box of paints open; after squeezing them on to your palette, leave the tops off so that they are ready for immediate use when required. If you are able to afford a standard paint-box, it is a useful asset, but not essential equipment to start with. You can perfectly well keep your tubes in a cardboard box and your brushes in a jar.

Now to begin our painting.

Squeeze some flake white on to your palette an inch or so from the container, and a small amount of ivory black near to it. Pour a little turpentine and a few drops of copal oil medium into the container. Using a small brush, No. 2 or No. 3, take some of each paint and mix them to form a pale grey. Only a very little black is necessary. Use only a drop of medium, mix the two paints vigorously together, thus keeping the mixture thin, rather than by adding medium which makes the paint too runny. A pale grey will show up clearly on the white canvas.

Now that the composition is planned, you can start at the top. This time you are concentrating on accuracy, measuring with your eye the exact distances and shapes. A brush can do quite different things from a piece of charcoal, and the look and feel of the work is of different character.

In Fig. 3 you will see how far to take this phase. From the very start your feelings are involved as well as your intellect. Your intellect should be used to put down the hard facts, judge the exact distances and the scientific accuracy of the drawing. Your feelings should be expressed in the way you use your brush to indicate these facts. Where an edge is hard and clear, as for instance the side of the book or the top of the lemon, your touch should be firm; where the edge is lost in shadow, as on the right side of the bowl, it should be more softly indicated. Not weakly or inaccurately, but with a lighter pressure of the brush. Modeling and cast shadows should be lightly suggested except in their very darkest parts, and then by not making the mixture of paint darker, but by a firmer pressure of the brush and a little added paint.

This whole operation should take about half an hour. If you are unsure of your drawing, you may naturally allow yourself longer, not to take this phase further in detail, but to see that it is accurate. Your whole painting will be based on the steel girders you are now putting up. This analogy is a good one; from another point of view, you might call it a blueprint.

Now we use color for the first time.

Remove the ivory black and clean the grey off your palette. Squeeze out your paints in the order I suggested in Chapter 2, about half an inch apart from each other. Do not be mean with the amounts and be sure to put out a big gob of flake white.

Our first aim is to cover the white canvas with paint as intelligently and as rapidly as we can. Only when the white canvas is covered, can we make the most reliable judgments.

Our procedure is, as usual, based on logical thinking. Because we want to match one color value against another, it is a good thing to choose a spot where two or three color values meet. This could be at the top of the bowl, where the background, book and bowl come together, or at the bottom, where the lemon, bowl and foreground touch one another. I suggest the first alternative because the background exerts an influence on all the color values it adjoins, and therefore makes a good point of departure.

Let us mix a tone for the background as it appears at the top of the bowl, remembering for the moment it can be only approximate and will have to be judged next to the color value of the book and the bowl. In rapid succession, we must make attempts at these three tones, our immediate aim being to relate them accurately to each other.

To make the creamy grey background, mix some ivory black, flake white and a little yellow ochre. Compare the mixture to the background, and mix the ingredients until you feel you have got the right tone. If it is a little too cool, add the tiniest bit of cadmium red; if too warm perhaps a touch of cobalt is needed. Remember, the "warmest" color is red and the "coolest" blue.

Having mixed your approximate background tone, brush it firmly and thinly on to the canvas to fill a small area enclosed on two sides by the top of the bowl and the side of the book. You cannot be certain how accurate your attempt has been. It may look too dark against the white canvas, or you may have made it too light because the background appears light to your eye against the darker bowl. Leave it for the moment and mix the blue for the book. This may possibly be composed of cobalt blue, combined with white, a touch of yellow ochre and maybe some ivory black. Brush some of this right up to and *touching* the painted background, leaving no white canvas showing between them at all. You will already be able to make a judgment between the background and the book. Mix some green as it appears on the lid of the bowl next to the background and paint it to touch the background and book.

Now you are in a position to judge the result and compare the grey, blue and green color values to one another. You may feel they need to be stronger or weaker, lighter or darker, as the case may be. It is most important that these colors should be correctly related.

At this stage, you should be "scrubbing" the paint on thinly, *not* thinned by too much medium, but by vigorous mixing. In the early stages of a painting, "scrubbing" is the best way to cover the canvas rapidly. With a brush not too heavily loaded with paint, rub or scrub it *hard* on to the canvas. The white canvas will make itself felt through to some extent. This keeps all your values, for the present, on the light side. Later on, you can paint more thickly, lay on your brush strokes more carefully and make the color values stronger. For the moment, you should concentrate on making them relatively true to one another.

The background and book are flat planes, and do not change their value very much for quite large areas. The bowl is quite a different problem. Not only do the green values constantly change, but the highlights on the shiny surface reflect the light from the window, becoming almost white, and in the shadow you can see reflections of the blue book and the yellow lemon. It is necessary for us to simplify these problems to begin with.

First of all extend the areas already painted of the background and the book. The background touches the bowl on the left side all the way down to the table. Scrub this part in, revealing the edge of the bowl as you do so. The book touches the bowl, too, on the other side, but very soon the blue becomes darker in the shadow cast by the bowl. Mix this darker value now and scrub it on where the shadow of the book comes, thus forming the edge of the bowl on the right side. Then continue along the edge of the lemon. See where the table begins on either side and scrub in some reddish tone on the foreground.

There are five separate color values which we must now consider in the bowl. In reality there are more, but we must approach them by stages.

1. The green on the surface facing the light
2. The half tone as the surface recedes from the light
3. The darkest shadow
4. The reflected light in the shadow
5. The highlights

Begin by scrubbing on some of the green already mixed and cover the area of the upper and middle portion of the bowl facing the light. Then mix a darker value, maybe by adding some more blue, yellow, black or burnt sienna, as well as some white to give it body. Scrub it on and *into* the edge of the green already there, keeping your eye on the rounded formation of the bowl. Now mix some still darker value, and extend it right across the bowl until it touches the book and the lemon. You should now have covered the bowl entirely.

Now judge the light tone of the highlights and place them *into* the green paint in their correct places. They may require a mixture of white and a touch of cobalt. Finally mix an appropriate tone to suggest the reflection in the shadow and paint it *into* the dark part. Be sure to keep the reflection low in tone; it probably gives the illusion of being lighter than it actually is, because it is surrounded by very dark tones.

Now paint the warm shadow cast by the cover of the book on the leaves inside, the further edge of the book cover, the value of the background in the shadow cast by the book, and the cast shadows on the foreground.

By this time everything should be covered except the lemon. Paint the lemon in exactly the same manner as you did the bowl. The red foreground will warm the underside, and the halftones will be greenish, the effect of the cool light on the yellow surface. Use lemon yellow and a little cadmium yellow and white for the yellowest portions, but notice how little of the surface is really pure yellow. If your surrounding values are satisfactory, the lemon should begin to stand out brightly.

Now your canvas should be almost painted over. There may be areas of the background or foreground which still need covering, but you should have a fair suggestion of reality; paler, rougher and simpler than it will eventually become, but nevertheless approaching the truth.

Time now enters our calculations, as it always must in oil painting. You have completed "Operation Covering the Canvas," and you may have taken two hours to do this. It is certainly time to rest and study the results.

When you are sufficiently relaxed, it is an excellent thing to continue to paint *into* the wet surface for at least another hour. If you have the time and the energy you could even attempt to finish the painting at one sitting. Should you not have enough time at your disposal, it is better to leave it than attempt a new phase of development that you cannot complete. Each phase must have its purpose, and that purpose must be completed before stopping work for the day.

The advantage of continuing at least for a time into the wet paint is tremendous. So far, you have been painting on a dry canvas, and had the disadvantage of a white surface on which to make your judgments. Many of these judgments will of necessity have been faulty. Now is the chance to improve and develop what you have done, with the agreeable wet paint to work into, and color values already there to guide you to more accurate decisions. Instead of having to go step by step judging one color value against the one immediately next to it, you are now master of any part of the canvas and can see the picture as a whole.

Edges are extremely important. An edge is where one color value meets another. Every edge must be considered separately. For instance, between half-tone and shadow where one value merges into the next, the edge is soft, but where the book touches the background, the edge is fairly hard and clearly defined. By our understanding and treatment of edges, we create a feeling of realism and of atmosphere and space surrounding the objects. Edges help to suggest the form, texture and character of the object; whether it is hard or soft, rough or smooth. No edges should be left unconsidered. That is one of the reasons why it is so important to continue working into the wet paint; you were so busy on the first round, you did not have time to think of them carefully enough.

Now that all the values have been placed on the canvas, you have the opportunity of judging not only the ones that immediately touch one another, but those that are some distance apart, and must also be related. Is the highlight on the bowl lighter than the highlight on the lemon? Is the shadow cast by the lemon on the foreground as dark as the one cast by the book? You are creating a new world on the canvas, and certain laws have to be obeyed within that world. I have intentionally chosen a simple group. When you paint a more elaborate one, you will realize even more clearly how every part of the picture is related to every other part. From now on, whether you decide to have a second session or not, improve the truth of your values and be sure that you leave no hard edges, except where they are required.

Avoid "no-man's lands"—bits of white canvas left where you have not had the courage to make one color touch another. Your extreme darks and lights should be held in reserve, as well as anything that could be called detail. Complicated reflected lights on the bowl are also kept back till near the end.

If you decide to finish the painting another day, be sure the surface is completely dry before you paint over it. Your immediate purpose, when you begin the second session is to go over the whole painting once more. Do not be afraid of losing or spoiling what is already there. The function of the first session was to be the foundation for the next day's work. You must have the courage to use the first day's work as a stepping stone to greater truth and accuracy of judgment.

At first, judge one value next to the one touching it as before, but as you progress, you can move more freely over the different areas. You might start by re-stating the background and then enriching the darker parts of the group so that your range of tone is at once extended. Do not hesitate to paint right across your highlights of yesterday and then re-state them more accurately and brilliantly. You are not *altering* or trying to make wrong right. You are making good better. When the painting is wet, pause once again to consider the work as a whole. Decide where your darkest darks come, as well as your lightest lights. Make them as rich and strong as required. Emphasize or soften edges as needed. Search for the reflected lights for more interesting color values. Suggest any surface markings such as lettering on the label on the book.

By choosing this small group of three objects, I have tried to keep the problems down to a minimum, but you will find them more than enough to begin with. Later on, you may want to try a more difficult arrangement, to help you improve your powers of observation and differentiate between subtle changes of values.

To this end, put together a group of objects such as a silver jug, a white plate, an egg and a glass tumbler against a grey background and on a white tablecloth, with perhaps one brightly colored object, such as a flower for contrast. It is your job as a painter to distinguish carefully between the subtle differences of value, and search for the delicate nuances between one color and another.

You must also learn to judge the contrasting values between a number of brilliant colors, as for example when painting flowers. There are many dangers to guard against, not the least being that flowers are "pretty" and may flatter you into thinking you are making a better job of them than you really are. As they are usually bright in color, you can easily be led astray and find yourself merely "coloring" them instead of carefully relating one value to another.

When you paint your first flower piece, arrange a few flowers casually, but agreeably in a simple vase and place them on a table against a fairly dark background. Start, as always, by painting the background up to and a little over where the flowers will come. Paint the green of the leaves and hold back your brilliant colors as long as possible; they will then tell out with all the more force. Try to finish the painting in one session, as flowers change so much from day to day. If this cannot be done, then complete whatever flowers you decide to paint and leave the others a mere suggestion to be continued next time.

6 *Approach to Landscape:* I

There are many different approaches to landscape painting. I shall describe one of these in detail, and discuss several in general. The Impressionists, such as Monet and Renoir, and the Post-Impressionists Cezanne, Gauguin and Van Gogh, still exert great influence on landscape painting today. What is good is never old-fashioned. Their immediate forerunners, Constable and Turner, also used methods that cannot be ignored.

One of your difficulties today is that you have too many examples to influence you. To learn a good method from start to finish is an excellent way to find what suits your temperament best.

Once you are out-of-doors the light factor, which we deliberately limited in our studio with a north light, becomes of the greatest importance. Light produces the most exciting and stimulating effects. Dawn, sunset, the brilliance of midday, the softness of dusk are all effects of light. Sky and sunlight dominate the scene. The sun moves across the sky, clouds of every shape and color float by and change the appearance of the scene as you watch. What we have to do, therefore, is to decide which aspect of the many-changing scene we wish to interpret. Whichever you choose, you still have to build your picture on a solid foundation, and use a technique which allows you to select what is necessary to make a good composition.

The method I shall describe is based on the idea that in front of nature, under what must always be difficult and changing conditions, it is impossible to paint more than a rapid sketch successfully. This rapid sketch can be the essence, the inspiration, of a larger and more carefully conceived work carried out in the studio later in your own time.

If light and color change rapidly, form does not. It is possible to return to the same spot and draw the scene with as much care and for as long as you wish. Your finished picture is therefore based on a quick color sketch which has caught the vital moment, plus a careful drawing of the permanent topography of the scene.

In certain climates, as in the South of France, the weather is fairly constant, but even there the sun does not stand still. Some Impressionists completed their pictures out-of-doors, returning to the same spot each day at the same time, working for an hour or so, sometimes painting several pictures at different times during the same day. The method I am going to describe is the one in which you attempt to seize the moment within an hour or even less, building up your finished picture at home.

When studying still life as an exercise to learn painting, you were not allowed to compromise with tricks or short cuts. When it comes to painting out-of-doors, you must use every trick at your disposal to overcome the practical difficulties involved. You want to get the maximum effect in the minimum of time. You are trying to catch your excitement and emotion in the passing moment.

What is it that makes you want to paint a landscape? The most obvious answer is to record the beauty of a scene, but there is far more to it than that. Do we mean the beauty of a pretty view, the grandeur of a sunset, the architectural glory of New York or Venice, or the suddenly revealed effect of light through an archway as seen by you alone. There can be the beauty of the scene itself, but what is far more important, there is the beauty you discover for yourself and which only you can reveal to others. This is the heart of the matter. Any gifted amateur can imitate a "picturesque" view, but this is not seeing beauty, merely recording an attractive scene which has pleasant associations for the onlooker. What the good landscape artist must do is to let his personal vision guide him to his subject. Many artists are happiest in surroundings they know best, where they have had ample opportunity for studying the scenes in every mood and at every season of the year. You must be guided to your subject by what you love and what stirs you emotionally. This may be the color values of a row of tenement buildings or a range of stark, bleak hills against a turbulent sky.

Let us now be practical. Van Gogh carried his canvas and easel on his back, trudging for miles in the burning sun—but then he went mad. Today most of us have the use of a car to carry our equipment. You will need a light, folding easel—although the lid of a paint box is usually fitted to carry a canvas board and may suffice. A folding stool is necessary, and beyond that you can suit yourself in what you consider necessary for your comfort.

Your range of color out-of-doors will be wider, so you will need some cerulean blue and extra shades of cadmium yellows and oranges.

It is best to use a toned canvas or canvas board, or a prepared wooden panel. The tone can be a warm, tobacco brown, or neutral dark grey. The practical advantage of this is that your color scheme soon becomes united by its all-pervading tone, and your lights and bright colors tell out immediately against the darker brown. This saves the time necessary to build up to them, as we had to in painting the still life on a white canvas.

Traditionally, there is a foreground, middle distance and distance. Just as in the still life, where you put one object in front of another, so in landscape you conceive a picture in depth. A feeling of recession is one of the important elements in a good landscape.

In your sketch, you must let the impulse that moves you have full freedom to express itself. You don't have to bother too much about accuracy of drawing, because you can return later for careful study. All the same, the sketch should contain the vital elements of the finished picture. If the subject has architectural features such as a church or a bridge, it is wiser to spend a certain time fixing their position with some degree of accuracy. You must develop a time sense that will allow you to know just how long can be spent on the various essential preliminaries.

> To begin your sketch, which should be approximately 9 x 7 or 12 x 10, draw in the main features of a landscape with a brush in the same way that you did the still life, like a topographical map. Just as you had then to establish where the table had to be placed, you must now decide where the horizon will come. Draw in the main features of the scene with a small brush, No. 2 or No. 3. Pay particular attention to the relation of the sky to the rest of the landscape, that plays such a dominant part in any picture.

Landscape painters who lived in flat countries such as Holland or East Anglia have often made the sky their chief subject. Constable, Turner and

Monet loved to paint clouds. Cezanne and Van Gogh used the blue sky of Provence to the greatest advantage. All landscape painters are fascinated by the constantly changing drama of the sky.

The brilliant British contemporary artist, John Piper, has added immeasurably to the drama of his pictures by using threatening dark grey clouds behind his sunlit castles and hills. A charming story is told of how he was commissioned to paint a series of famous country houses. The pictures were later inspected by a Very Eminent Personage who remarked: "Very nice indeed, Mr. Piper, what a pity you had such bad weather!"

This little story is a significant one. It reveals the attitude of so many people to painting in general. It is virtually impossible for them to escape from the subject and association of the scene depicted. It is essential to understand the difference between the mere surface imitation of nature and the interpretation of your own feelings. Turner, one of the greatest landscape painters who ever lived, saw nature as an immense theatre where wind and waves, mountains and valleys, sunlight and shadow played an eternal melodrama. When I see a sketch painted spontaneously on the spot, I like to feel at once what it was that moved the artist to choose that particular aspect of the scene. This, to me, is more important than careful photographic accuracy.

> After drawing your main features with a brush, paint in the general value of the sky and immediately judge the value of the buildings, trees, hills of whatever is immediately touching the sky, against it. Keep in mind that the contrast of light and shadow will be greater on the objects as they approach the foreground, just as the color will be more intense. There should be one or more centers of particular interest—focal points of drama where a white cloud reveals a church tower, a gleam of water is surrounded by dark foliage, or a red roof stands out as accent. Feel for these as soon as possible. Your unifying background will help to hold the sketch together and allow you to place significant accents much sooner than if you use the white foundation.

The actual range of tones of a landscape in sunlight as seen by the eye, is far greater than can be literally expressed in paint between its extremes of black and white. It is therefore necessary to create the illusion of brilliance. Many artists have been fascinated by this problem, particularly the Impressionists and the Post-Impressionists. The classical method was to contrast very dark trees or buildings against the light sky and achieve an effect of sunlight behind them. The shadows were painted dark brown or black and sometimes tended to make the pictures somber and lacking in color. The Impressionists devised a method of painting light, not only by using more color in the shadows, making them full of blues and purples, but of breaking up the lights into their prismatic components, bright pinks, yellows, greens and blues, filling their pictures with the effect of sunshine. Renoir was a master of this technique and Monet, Pissarro and Sisley, all experimented successfully with effects of light. The Pointillists, Seurat and Signac, worked out a scientific method of painting in small colored dots which at a distance merged together and created an illusion of light as seen out-of-doors. Van Gogh was obsessed by sunshine and achieved the effect of brilliance by loading on pigments in primary colors.

> Make up your mind which is to be the brightest spot in your picture and subordinate everything else to this in key. A cloud, a white sail, or sunshine reflected on a white building, might even be painted in pure white. Decide where your darkest shadow will come and make it as richly dark as necessary. Your range of tones will fall between these two extremes. On a dull day, your normal palette should encompass the range of color values without difficulty. Remember that if you want a color to appear particularly bright, it is a good thing to surround it with lower tones.

Two major colors tend to dominate landscapes, green and blue. Blue is best revealed when surrounded by other colors. Too much blue in any area defeats its own purpose and becomes monotonous. A patch of blue in the sky can create a wonderful effect when encircled by the subtle greys of clouds. The blues in water tell out significantly against rich dark greens and browns. Even an expanse of intensely blue sky is made more effective by greenish, yellowish or purplish values as it nears the horizon. Be sparing and selective with blue and it will add greatly to the charm of your work.

Green is the most prevalent color in nature. There is an endless variety of shades of green from brilliant emerald to warm olive, from the rich shadows of an oak tree to the tender tones of a young leaf. One of your problems is how to prevent the prevalence of green becoming monotonous and to avoid painting too much "spinach."

Every landscape artist has developed his own technique for painting trees, from the architectural reconstructions of Cezanne, to the blurry fuzz of Corot. Search for the two or three important color values when painting a tree or group of trees and simplify their form. There is no time for further elaboration. If the trunks or a few heavy branches are visible, by all means make a note of them. In winter or early spring, the shapes of trees are revealed in all their structural beauty and make fascinating patterns against the sky. Think of the tree, or group of trees, as a whole, as large forms revealed by the light from the sky or the sun above. If there are several trees, search for the difference in character between them, both in color and form. The edges will reveal their leafiness sufficiently; make no attempt at any kind of detail beyond studying the edges. When painting buildings, keep your mind on their basic architectural forms, their essential boxlike nature, the sloping planes of the roofs, the receding planes of the walls.

> When you have covered your small canvas boldly with sky, distance, middle distance and foreground, making certain you study their true color relationships, you might take a small brush and add a few touches to bring out any striking accents, some architectural detail, a delicate edge of trees, some brilliant note of flowers, or to introduce a suggestion of human beings. Your sketch must be full of significant facts, so that when you use it for reference later on, it will immediately stir your memory.

You may find that your rapid sketches are becoming charming little pictures in their own right and you may not want to bother to use them for the basis of a bigger picture. If they have caught the effect of a passing moment, nothing could be better. There are two things to be warned against. Do not attempt to "improve" on them in the studio. Do not return to the same spot and try to take them further. This is absolutely fatal. If you are enjoying particularly steady weather, you can plan to paint a scene on consecutive days under similar conditions at the same hour, building up the sketch as you did the still life, so that your first day's work is a preparation for a more fully developed second painting and even possibly, a third. Circumstances do not often allow for this and most climates vary so much from day to day that it is impossible to expect the same conditions. I have many times seen artists painting busily at their easels on pictures long after the light has changed and their work looks heavy and lifeless.

7 Approach to Landscape: II

In the two pictures on page VIII of the picture insert, we have the perfect example of the method I am suggesting. The fact that they were painted by John Constable over a hundred years ago, makes them not one whit less useful today. They are invaluable as an illustration of a logical, exciting, workable method. It is obvious that the sketch was done at one sitting. Constable has seized on the dramatic silhouette of the houses and mill on the left, with the church tower making an interesting focal point against the mass of bright cloudy sky. In the middle foreground, the water makes a pleasing pattern of light and shade with the white foam as a light accent and the sail forming an amusing shape, while to the right, are some interesting forms of woodwork. All this is boldly and dramatically expressed at white heat. Constable painted many hundreds of such sketches and today they are even more appreciated than at the time they were painted. They are completely spontaneous and unselfconscious expressions of the artist's personal feelings.

Now look at the "finished" picture developed from the germ of the sketch. Constable has painted a balanced, elaborate and sensitive work of art. This has the poetry of emotion recollected in tranquillity. Gone is the dash and fire of the sketch. In exchange we have a planned picture built up with the greatest care, a complex pattern of form and color which, in spite of its intricate structure of elaborate surface detail, retains the feeling of simplicity and the peaceful spirit of the English countryside the artist loved so well.

Without doubt, before beginning the larger painting, he returned to the spot many times and made careful drawings of the mill, the lock, the church and the trees. It was the fashion in 1840 to exhibit big "Academy" pictures, painstakingly painted in every detail. Constable rose above this merely slavish imitation and because he was a fine artist, used his taste and discretion in merging detail into the larger design. No artist can fully escape from the age he lives in and some people find his finished pictures a little over-romantic in the Victorian style. But no one today could quarrel with his quick sketches which remain as vital as the day they were painted, causing us to share in his excitement and joy in the world around him.

Just as Constable's bigger pictures belong to the period of 1840, when it was the "modern" and accepted thing to paint large landscapes, so today, we have a "modern" approach and prefer pictures that do not adopt such a literal transcription of nature. There has been a complete revolution since that time. If we wish to paint landscape with a contemporary eye, there is still no reason why we should not use Constable's general method of approach which was logical and workmanlike and used by many artists at different periods.

Now we must consider how to plan a picture using our color sketch as a stimulating starting point. Walter Sickert never based the structure of his picture on the color sketch but on a drawing done on the same spot, carried out with less haste, which more accurately showed the structural forms. You can see how Constable reorganized his scene, introducing a sailing boat, horses, a tree stump and so on, to make a far more complex arrangement. This complicated development needs great experience and artistic perception. Sickert maintained, rightly or wrongly, that unless a picture had been filtered through the intellectual processes of the mind, it could not be seriously considered as a work of art. This is a debatable point. There are many examples of fine painting, including our little Constable sketch, which were painted at white heat and can be considered seriously as works of artistic value. Both Manet and Monet painted many lovely sketches which are works of art in their own right. Van Gogh painted most of his later and most famous pictures at fever pitch, so it is not wise to make general assertions about the ultimate value of a particular method. A fine artist can paint rapidly with all his conscious and subconscious knowledge pouring forth to create a miracle. Degas and Cezanne are examples of painters who preferred to work on their finished pictures slowly and quietly by a process of selection and rejection. Sickert himself looked on his sketches more as a workman's notes than as pictures. I believe it is best to make your sketches rapidly and spontaneously, then come home and study them quietly. When you feel that you are capable of building up a considered picture, choose a sketch which pleases you and retains the spark of emotion you felt at the time. Return to the spot, take your sketch with you and make a careful study of the scene in pencil, using a sketch book or block of cartridge paper, and write down any notes of a descriptive nature to help you increase your store of knowledge. Use your color sketch only to remind you of your original impressions and to show what you will still need to know or what you may have omitted to note in your natural haste. By all means make your color sketch and drawing on the same occasion if time permits.

When you come to paint your picture at home, take time to think about what you are trying to achieve. Sickert's ideal was to paint a picture which gave the air of complete spontaneity but was, in fact, extremely carefully planned to give just that effect. If you are a painter with your own ideas, you will plan according to your personal outlook. My aim is not to make you imitate Sickert or Constable, but to help you create a picture the way you feel it, using their logical program as a guide.

> Decide first of all on the scale you wish to adopt, being careful not to plan it too large for the content. If your drawing is 9 x 7, you could make your picture 18 x 14, or you might prefer a larger one, 36 x 28. "Square-up" your drawing, which consists of a network of squares conveniently placed about an inch apart. Do the same proportionately on the large canvas, in charcoal (pencil tends to show through oil paint). This time a white canvas is best. Fix the lines lightly and rub off the superfluous charcoal. Now re-draw onto your canvas the chief features of the drawing using the squares as your guide, and if necessary, numbering them across the top and down the side to help you. Keep the drawing light and suggestive, using a pointed piece of charcoal, just as you did in the still life.

Now is the time to consider what changes you want to make that depart in some way from the original drawing, so as to make the design simpler, stronger and more interesting. There may be some dramatic feature of the color sketch you wish to incorporate, or an additional element, such as a figure or other new motif. Now that you are working on a larger scale, you should stand back, look at the canvas thoughtfully, visualize how it will appear when finished, and consider whether the larger area will allow for further elaboration of content and if so, how much. Eliminate inessentials which interfere with the basic design and let the color sketch remind you of your original impulse; be sure it does not get smothered by unimportant detail.

Take a brush and suggest very lightly the larger masses of light and shade so that you can get a "preview" of the finished picture. For this purpose a pale mixture of white and venetian red is very pleasant. Grey or pale green can be used if preferred. The venetian red gives a warm effect which will show through the predominantly cooler tones of blues and greens.

Sickert advocated painting a complete monochrome in a pale warm color on which to found a landscape. He used pure white for the lightest portions and even the darkest parts were painted in a pale tone. If the scale is kept light it is surprising how effective the result can look and the great advantage is that it prevents the over-painting from becoming heavy.

A convenient practice that Sickert used, was to place four or five gobs of white paint on the palette, and then add very small amounts of venetian red, a little more to each one, so that his values were graded down from pure white to pale red. He then boldly scrubbed on the different tones where required, using white with considerable thickness. This gave body and a quality of richness to the paint.

There is no reason to hurry over this preparatory foundation; it can be kept broad and simple—or developed to some degree of finish. When you feel you have taken it far enough, give it time to dry completely. If your paint is fairly thick it may need as long as a week before the rich white portions are fully dry. Use only just enough medium to allow the paint to move with reasonable freedom; a mixture of turpentine and a small quantity of copal or linseed oil is best. Be sure that the drawing is used as your chief guide although your color sketch may be at hand to give you further ideas.

Now begin the first application of color using your color sketch for reference. Because true color relationships are difficult to judge when first placed on a pale ground, it is important to get the canvas covered with the new surface of color as soon as possible. Start by brushing in the sky, much as you did in the sketch—and then relate the tones immediately next to it. You may find that painting over pure white makes your light colors seem temporarily less light, but once the white is eliminated it will be easier to judge the new relationships.

Sickert, being a direct descendant of the Impressionists, advised you to search carefully for the color of your half-tones and shadows. He wanted you to make a decision whether a tone was more blue, purple, green or red rather than neutral grey or brown.

The Impressionists worked on the theory that the effect of light out-of-doors could be re-created only by intensifying the colors on the canvas. Their brilliant pictures, following a period when landscapes tended to be dark and heavy, fully justified their theory. It was they who first broke away from a tradition of formal, classical landscapes manufactured in the studio. They based their paintings on their immediate response to nature. In England, Constable and Turner were the forerunners of this movement, but it was the Impressionists who first introduced a prismatic scheme of color that had never been used before, especially in bigger pictures. Constable still tended to paint brown shadows in his "finished" paintings.

Try to cover the monochrome with color in one session. If the canvas is too large for you to attempt this, decide on one portion, say the left half and get the relative values reasonably accurate. The next day complete the other half so that both halves are now united in one scheme. Before continuing further, take a long and thoughtful look at what you have done so far and be searching in your criticism of its design and structure. See where you can simplify the pattern and eliminate inessentials. Plan where your accents are going to come using your color sketch for inspiration and your own mind and personal ideas as a controlling influence. Remember that sky and clouds can be modified to suit your purpose, and trees and architecture elaborated if necessary or kept severely simple. Let the eye of the onlooker be led towards the interesting parts and see that the focus of dramatic interest is emphasized. From now on you must develop your picture much as you did the still life, making it gradually stronger and more colorful until the spirit of the sketch is recaptured, the structure and content of the drawing fully used, and your own ideas satisfactorily expressed.

All this may sound very difficult and complicated—and so it is! For a time you may be satisfied with your sketches alone. Then your powers of observation will increase and you will feel that there is more you want to express. You may wish to dispense with the monochrome and start painting in color immediately after drawing with the brush. There are certain advantages to this approach, such as a bolder attack and greater speed. But you must be sure you are not merely making a larger reproduction of your color sketch. The whole point of doing a picture in the studio is the immense advantage of unlimited time to work under comfortable conditions. However, if you feel you have planned your larger picture sufficiently well from your drawing, you may start right away with color. One danger is that if you go on too long you may lose the feeling of freshness. Painting a monochrome underneath does separate the two problems of form and color.

Cezanne devised a careful analytical method by which he built up his landscapes in a solid architectural manner in pure color, using each brush stroke significantly to form separate planes and create an illusion of recession by different color values. His great achievement was to use the heightened color of the Impressionists and combine it with strong solid form. There had been a danger that too much atmospheric haziness and diffused sunlight would become formless and that Impressionism would degenerate into woolliness. Cezanne rightly maintained that the great art of the past had been based on a solid foundation of architectural design. Few have since quarreled with the idea.

Most beginners are influenced by artists who make a particular appeal to them. This is in many ways a good thing and much can be gained by following, for a time, the work of a great painter. One danger to guard against is a tendency to imitate superficial mannerisms. I often amuse myself at an exhibition by noticing under whose influence the various pictures have been painted. Usually there are several watered-down Picassos, Cezannes, Renoirs or Van Goghs. Great artists quite naturally influence lesser ones. What is important is to learn something from their approach to design, color and form, rather than their surface effects and personal idiosyncracies. Van Gogh has had a very bad effect on many artists who only imitate his violence and his loading on of bright colors. These characteristics were the natural development of his particular temperament and he succeeded in creating a work of art by the intensity of his personal vision and not by tricks of technique. A powerful and dynamic personality like Picasso has influenced almost every contemporary painter whether he realizes it or not. His original ideas and immense creative imagination have covered every aspect of painting. It is clear that his early work was influenced by the Impressionists, especially Toulouse-Lautrec and Degas, until he achieved complete freedom of personal expression. His fine draughtsmanship has given even his most daring experiments a firm structural basis. Beginners should remember this when attempting to work under his influence.

Artists such as Rousseau le Douanier or Grandma Moses represent another approach to painting, the gifted amateur whose work rises above the ordinary by imaginative power and original conception, even though limited by lack of training and technical skill. Grandma Moses owes her claim to serious consideration, not only because of the naive charm of her delightful record of New England life, but because she is a born colorist and has a splendid sense of pattern due to her long experience of embroidery. Her inability to create solid forms is overcome by her refusal to attempt more than she can accomplish. Instead of failing to achieve solidity she succeeds in giving her flatness a charm of its own.

If you employ the general method I have described, you can still choose whether you want to express your own feelings entirely or work for a time under the influence of an admired master. There is nothing in the program that ties you down to painting in any particular style. It allows you to express yourself with the greatest freedom, merely giving you signposts to guide you through difficult country. The important points to remember are that you should paint rapidly in front of nature to capture the passing moment by means of essential color relationships, and rely on drawings and notes for accuracy and detail. It is illogical to continue painting when the original scene has changed. A finished picture should be painted at leisure in the studio, the only alternative being to return to the same spot if conditions are similar from day to day.

8 Approach to Portrait Painting: I

To paint a portrait well, you must not only be an experienced painter, but interested in character and psychology. Portrait painting is specially difficult because a new element, entirely separated from painting, is involved. The subtle and elusive qualities that go to form "expression" and "likeness" are as difficult to catch as the proverbial butterfly. It is possible to paint an excellent study of a head yet miss the likeness. It is also possible to get an excellent likeness in an otherwise poor painting.

It is unwise to attempt a portrait without having learned the elements of painting first; if you try to, the result will almost certainly be disastrous. I have seen many such efforts and when I entreat beginners to start with still life, they say it is "boring" and they are only interested in portraits. Still life is far from boring when approached in the right spirit and, until you have understood the handling of your medium and some of the problems of form and color, you cannot hope to paint a successful portrait.

Painting a portrait involves another human being. You have to talk to him, amuse him and get to know him. At the same time your mind must be working at top speed dealing with modeling, color relationships and all the various technical problems of painting. How can you hope to do this if you are inexperienced? Features such as the eyes and mouth attract too much attention from the beginner. Modeling is either over-done, causing the sitter to look older and plainer, or under-done, in which case the face looks flat and empty. If the color values are not true, the face looks "dirty." If the edges are poor, it looks hard. A successful portrait should, by definition, be sympathetic, so that lack of technical knowledge may make it look hard, old and dirty, causing embarrassment all round.

In my book *Practical Portrait Painting,* I have dealt with all aspects of the subject. Here I shall describe the process I use myself and warn you of the many pitfalls that await you. All beginners make the same mistakes. As it seems impossible to avoid them, I will attempt to help you out of the traps in which you will inevitably fall. Let me assume that you have painted for some months and have a working knowledge of drawing and painting. There are certain physical conditions necessary before you begin to paint a portrait.

> You must have a good north light and enough space in which to work freely. The light should fall over your shoulder on to the model and your canvas, enabling you to see both clearly. There should be sufficient space for you to walk back several feet to observe your work at a distance. You should stand at your easel and have the sitter raised on a platform so that his head is at eye level. These conditions will be found in any normal "studio," but if you have to work at home, you must find a room, due north, with a window the top of which is at least 10 feet above the floor level and shows a view of the sky uninterrupted by houses or trees. If you are cramped for space or have to paint sitting down, or the light is changeable or inadequate, your chances of success are poor.
>
> Here are some generalizations to remember: Because the desire to get a likeness is strong, it interferes with the normal progress of the painting. In essence the technical approach resembles the painting of still life. The surface detail has to be held back until the structure and form of the head and the color relationships of background, hair, face and clothes are truly established. If you put in the detail of features too soon, you become afraid to paint freely afterwards for fear of losing what you have so painstakingly established. This often causes a promising beginning to deteriorate as the painting progresses. The detail of the features should be painted as late as possible.

Another fault of the beginner is to think of hair, eyes, nose and mouth separately instead of all being intimately related. The features, structure and modeling of the face are all interwoven and individual parts should not be thought of by themselves but in relation to the face as a whole. It is important to remember that the head is basically egg-shaped and that smaller forms on the surface must be all related to the larger one. For instance, if the light is from above, no highlights can be stronger than the one on the forehead or the feeling of solidity will be lost.

If you are one of a group of students in a portrait class, you are not painting a portrait in the true sense at all. For obvious reasons it is not possible to carry on a conversation with the model and become acquainted with his character. The procedure is much the same, but when painting a portrait, you should become closely involved with the sitter and get a true understanding of his nature and study his constantly changing expression.

PROCEDURE FOR PAINTING A HEAD AND SHOULDERS PORTRAIT, size 16 inches x 20 inches

POSING AND LIGHTING:

Pose your sitter so that his most characteristic features and bone structure are revealed at their best.

Daylight coming from a certain height and falling over your left shoulder shows these up most clearly. Choose a front or three-quarter view. Be sure that the sitter is relaxed and if there is a slight turn to the head and shoulders, it helps to give a sense of movement and vitality to the portrait. If you wish the eyes in the picture to follow you, have the sitter looking directly at you. Avoid too much shadow on the face as well as too little, which may flatten the modeling. Stand with your canvas almost at right-angles to the window so that the wet paint will not reflect the light. Use a simple background, a screen hung with suitable material is convenient. Choose a piece of drapery in harmony with the coloring of your sitter. I usually use one light, enough to reveal the silhouette of the head.

PLACING THE HEAD ON THE CANVAS:

A picture can be spoiled by careless planning. Place the head about 1½ inches to 2 inches below the top of the canvas. If you put it any lower, the result will be unpleasing in a small picture. In a three-quarter view, do not cramp the head too far to one side of the picture. Use a piece of charcoal to indicate the general pose with special attention to the turn of the head on the neck, and the movement of the shoulders. Do not go into details of features which are best suggested later with a brush. You are placing the head and shoulders on the canvas only. If you are not happy with your first attempt do not hesitate to brush it off and have another try. Be absolutely sure that you have filled the space well and that the position and movement appear natural. When this has been satisfactorily carried out, fix your drawing lightly and brush off the superfluous charcoal leaving, as you did in the still life, just sufficient indication where to start painting, but nothing to tie you down to a hard map. Now that you are painting a living model, you must be prepared to adapt yourself to possible changes.

Once again, using the thin mixture of ivory black and flake white, to form a pale grey, make a light drawing of the head starting from the top. Use the brush sensitively, so that the nature of what you are painting is felt from the very first, softer edges for hair, harder ones for bone structure or crisp shadows. Take the greatest possible care to get the features and bone structure accurately stated in their right place and relation to one another, not painting them in any detail, but emphasizing certain vital points—the bone in the nose, the placing of the eyes and eyebrows, the edge of the cheekbone, the cast shadow under the nose and so on. This phase is of prime importance for you are putting up the steel girders of your construction which will have a direct influence on the progress and success of the whole portrait. It is better to take a whole sitting to do this correctly, rather than to rush the operation. When you are experienced it may not take more than half-an-hour to complete, but it must show a feeling for form and be absolutely reliable.

When you have completed this stage, the likeness should already be clearly there. If it is not, something is radically wrong and the fault must be traced to its source. I cannot impress on you enough the importance of a good foundation. My experience of teaching has shown me over and over again how careless most students are in the early stages of a portrait. It is not that they mean to be lazy, but that they are over-anxious to get on with the job. You may not discover that the foundation is unsound for several sittings and by that time you will be in real rouble. It is far more difficult to alter the structure of a portrait when it is nearly finished, and basic changes can seldom be done with much hope of success.

Let me be clear what I mean by accuracy. At this stage the distances between the features must be true, especially between the eyes, nose and mouth. The length of the nose must be right. The bone structure must be correctly drawn and the distance between the edge of the cheek and the nose and mouth strictly accurate. The general proportion of the head must be true and the placing of the ear and the way the head joins the neck and shoulders. If all these things are accurately placed the likeness will be apparent. *The triangle made by the two eyes and the tip of the nose is one of the basic facts in getting a likeness.* Check the length of the nose from the corner of the eye to the wing of the nostril. Show how the eyeball is placed inside the lids and the eye itself inside the bone structure. Model the eye as a whole, and be sure that the "further" eye in a three-quarter view does not stick out too far or the eye-ball appear to be popping out. I can only warn you of the things that most beginners do and beg you to correct them immediately if you find you have made the same errors. If all has gone well, then the "feel" of the sitter will be on the canvas and the essence of the character suggested. This will give you confidence to go on with color.

Many think it wise to begin painting a portrait in monochrome, so that the problem of form is tackled separately before the problem of color. This method was used almost entirely until the middle of the nineteenth century and is an excellent one from nearly every point of view. I have employed it myself on many occasions with success. The reasons I do not use it regularly are, firstly, it takes longer than the direct method, especially as the monochrome takes several days to dry before it can be painted over, and secondly, direct painting seems more in tune with my own temperament, which is essentially impatient. After I have described the direct method in some detail, I will give a brief summary of the indirect method of painting over a monochrome.

A portrait must be vital and fresh. It must also have depth of understanding and be a study of character, as well as of form and color. How best to combine these different elements? My plan is to use the first two or three sittings to feel my way, without using thick paint, strong contrast, bright color or sharp edges. I learn all I can about the form and color and structure of my sitter, without committing myself too much on canvas with thick pigment. By the third or fourth sitting I have become familiar with my sitter's character, and I let myself go with a full brush, rich pigment and true color values. When the paint is dry, I modify, simplify and add final accents where necessary.

ESTABLISHING COLOR VALUES:

Now it is time to put out your paints, in the same order as before. As in the still life, it should be your aim to cover the white canvas thinly in one sitting, or at least as much as you can in the time. If your grey drawing was put on sufficiently dry, it should remain in place even when you paint freely over it. If you have spent a whole sitting on the preliminaries, it will be quite dry when you start in color the next day.

Your first job is to relate the background to the hair. Mix a value for the background first and be sure you make a sufficient amount to cover the area immediately surrounding the whole head. Scrub it on thinly, right up to and over the edge of the hair and the other parts of the head and neck touching the background.

Now mix a value for the tone of the hair where it touches the background, beginning at a place where the silhouette is particularly clear, and paint it right up against and into the background, leaving no hard edges. Continue to paint the hair in two or three tones, taking care to keep the sense of light falling on the head, however dark the color of the hair may appear to be. At present you are keeping all the tones relatively lighter than nature, and if the hair is dark brown or black, it is best to keep the color very warm and thin in the dark parts during the first sitting so that it will glow through when you paint over it. The background may also vary in tone from one side to another. Use two or more brushes for the background and maybe three for the hair.

Re-state the background more accurately now that you can relate it to the hair. The process of painting is one of constantly developing true relationships between different values. If the hair is complicated by waves and curls, do *not* get involved in accidental surface forms at this point. Your aim is to cover the canvas as simply and intelligently as possible, selecting only the basic forms and relationships for the present.

Your plan is to surround the face. If the dress or collar comes up close to the neck, by all means suggest that as well. When painting the still life, the lemon was surrounded on all sides before being directly attacked; in the same way we are surrounding the flesh color of the face because it is the most difficult to judge. At last we are ready to do this. A good place to start is the area round the temple on the shadow side. It is the firm bone structure where two planes meet. One plane turns towards the light, the other away from it. You can judge the relative tone value against the hair immediately above. Mix the color for the flesh tone in shadow. This could be made of cadmium or indian red, viridian, a touch of yellow ochre and a little white. Scrub the mixture, when you are sure it is satisfactory, lightly over the whole of the plane that is turned away from the light, feeling your way round the temple, cheekbone to the jaw and chin, across to the hair, over the ear and down the side of the neck. Paint the shadow side of the nose, suggest the eyes and eyebrows, letting the grey underpainting guide you all the while. Paint thinly, pressing the paint on firmly. It will not require great depth of tone to show up against the white canvas. You should be developing the modeling and structure of the face with a tone that is neither too warm nor too cold.

Now mix a general flesh tone for the light areas. A little cadmium red, yellow ochre and white will probably suffice. Take a fairly big brush, and have the courage to scrub the paint over the whole of the light areas on both sides of the face and on the neck, using just a little medium and turpentine to thin the mixture which contains a fair amount of flake white. The grey structure will still show through, but the white canvas will have been covered. Do not hesitate to go right *over* the eyes and mouth, you will find it all the better to paint them into the wet surface. Avoid hard edges, but where the edge is clearly defined, as for instance against the cheekbone, see that it is well drawn.

Now that the whole area is wet, you can suggest the features more carefully. When you come to the eyebrows, remember they are not hard lines on the surface. See how they reflect the light and then become darker as they turn under the brow. Paint only what you can see clearly and make no attempt to search for detail. A few "signposts" will come in useful, the crisp shadow between the brow and the upper lid, the general color of the iris, the modeling under the eye. You might even suggest where the highlights will come later in the eyes, using a sable brush and a spot of white, which will immediately give the face a little life. These touches are of course merely preliminary. Do not let the whites of the eyes confuse you and make them too light; they are mostly shadowed either from the lids or by being turned away from the light, and in any case are a soft grey blue in color. Do not leave them as horrible white triangles, please!

The darker, cast shadows should be warm; the half-tones, where they merge into the light, cooler. Treat the mouth in a very tentative manner as it is bound to change a great deal. If the sitter uses lipstick, the merest suggestion of red will suffice for the moment. Record the fact that the upper lip is darker than the lower and paint the cool shadow under the lower lip. Notice how the corners of the mouth tuck into the cheeks. Paint the light area on the forehead and on the bridge and tip of the nose. See where the light catches the cheekbones. Take particular care where the cheek turns from shadow into light. The modeling here is vitally important and greatly influences the expression.

There will probably be a reflected light under the chin. A touch of cadmium yellow mixed in with your tone may give it the necessary glow. Do not get involved with the intricate modeling of the ear, or try to see too much into the shadow side. The best advice I can give is to remember: *The head is an egg.*

Sometimes, during a class I have fetched an egg and asked the model to hold it in his hand. This has clearly shown how similar they are, and helped

PORTRAIT OF EMIL DURANTY by Degas. A fine example of a "working" drawing—a study for a picture to be carried out later. It is vigorous but sensitive, catching the character of the sitter, both in action and expression. Degas was a master of line and accent, and selected only what was essential and significant. *Courtesy of the Metropolitan Museum of Art. Rogers Fund, 1918.*

STILL LIFE. The three objects in this group were chosen for their simple shapes and their difference in color and surface texture. In Chapter 5 I describe exactly how it was painted.

The first stage *(1)* was drawn lightly in charcoal, placing the objects in relation to one another and to the sides of the canvas. The second stage *(2)* was drawn with the brush in pale grey paint—not copying over the charcoal, but directly from the group.

The following six illustrations show how the painting developed. Starting at a point where the background is seen against the jar and the book, one value is judged against the one next to it. At first the paint was kept thin, and the values relatively light. Later exact color-values were built up, and thicker pigment used. The highest lights, darkest darks and strongest color were kept back until near the end.

(1)

(2)

(3)

(4)

(5)

(6)

(7)

(8)

(9)

MAN SEATED ON A STEP by Rembrandt. This brilliant study is another example of a great draughtsman's power of selecting essential forms, as well as the ability to catch pose and character in a rapid drawing. *Courtesy of the Metropolitan Museum of Art. Bequest of Mrs. H. O. Havemeyer, 1929. The H. O. Havemeyer Collection.*

MERRY JOSEPH BLONDEL by Ingres. This sensitive portrait drawing brings out the subtle modelling and the character of the sitter. Ingres has rejected anything that was accidental or unimportant. The drawing was, of course, completed as an end in itself. *Courtesy of the Metropolitan Museum of Art. Bequest of Grace Rainey Rogers. 1943.*

(1)

(2)

SIX STAGES OF A PORTRAIT. This portrait of a young man was painted to illustrate the method described in Chapters 8 and 9. The charcoal drawing *(1)* is done chiefly to establish the placing of the head and shoulders on the canvas, the general pose, and the position of the features. The drawing in grey paint *(2)* is done freshly from the model, and not copied over the charcoal. The four stages in color show the gradual development of the portrait after each sitting. Note how on the first day I concentrated on getting the color values truly related, but lighter than at the finish.

The second sitting is a development of the first, but still restrained. The third is a complete repainting; this time everything is in full color, and the features well defined.

The fourth shows how I was able to restate and emphasize certain facts that I had become familiar with, such as the characteristic shape of the hair. After the shirt was painted I was able to relate various accents and pull the whole portrait together.

(3)

(4)

(5)

(6)

Top. DEDHAM MILL by John Constable. Small oil-study for the bottom picture. Oil on paper. This brilliant sketch, painted at white heat in front of nature, is a record of Constable's feelings as well as a statement of what the scene looked like. It is a perfect example of how a quick color sketch contains the germ of a fine picture, besides being a small work of art itself.

Bottom. DEDHAM MILL, ESSEX by John Constable. Oil on canvas signed and dated 1820. Underneath we see the "finished" picture, completed in the studio, after Constable had worked out a balanced and complete composition at leisure. *Victoria and Albert Museum. Crown Copyright.*

LANDSCAPE WITH BARN by Rembrandt. This is the kind of drawing on which a large painting could be based. It is informative and full of significant facts, besides being a beautiful drawing in itself. *Courtesy of the Metropolitan Museum of Art. Bequest of Mrs. H. O. Havemeyer, 1929. The H. O. Havemeyer Collection.*

BIRTH OF ST. JOHN THE BAPTIST by Francesco Solimena. This elaborate and rather pretentious composition should be compared to the Vermeer, on the next page, which in its simplicity and subtlety is a far greater work of art. *Courtesy of the Metropolitan Museum of Art. Rogers Fund, 1906.*

WOMAN WITH A JUG by Vermeer. This small, jewel-like work of art contains the very essence of all that is beautiful and significant in painting. It is superb in color, completely satisfying in design, both on the surface and in depth, rich in quality of paint, and a wonderful example of the use of light. An analysis of its qualities appears in Chapter 10. *Courtesy of the Metropolitan Museum of Art. Gift of Henry G. Marquand, 1889.*

Top. CHRIST HEALING THE WOMAN WITH AN ISSUE OF BLOOD by Veronese. *Collection of the Kunsthistorisches Museum of Vienna. From a color slide by Francis G. Mayer.*

Right. INTERIOR AT NICE by Henri Matisse. *Collection of Mrs. Albert D. Lasker. Ektachrome by Francis G. Mayer.*

It is fascinating to compare this Veronese and Matisse. Although the subjects are so different, the color harmonies and composition are curiously alike. Notice the use of ochres, greys and blues, with red and orange accents. Compare the sweeping diagonal line upwards from lower left hand corner of the Veronese to the line of the curtain in the Matisse, as well as the stabilizing perpendicular columns in one and the upright panels in the other.

YOUNG GIRL AT AN OPEN HALF-DOOR by Rembrandt. A great picture from all points of view. A subtle and sensitive portrait, and a perfectly balanced composition, both in form and light and shade. The expression is tender and feminine but there are no concessions to mere prettiness. The design is bold and yet the picture is filled with mystery and atmosphere. *Courtesy of the Art Institute of Chicago. Mr. and Mrs. Martin A. Ryerson Collection.*

ABSINTHE DRINKERS by Degas. A highly original composition, which only a master of design could have invented. The eye is led up to the two characters along the edge of the tables. Who but Degas would have dared to place his center of interest in the top corner? Notice the way the objects on the tables are suggested, so that the interest in the figures is not disturbed. *Collection of the Louvre, Paris. Archives Photographiques.*

BEDROOM AT ARLES by Vincent Van Gogh. This is an example of how deep emotion and intensity of vision have been able to transform the painting of an ordinary room into a masterpiece. This is not only a view of Van Gogh's room, but a look into his mind and heart. *Courtesy of The Art Institute of Chicago, Helen Birch Bartlett Memorial Collection.*

Le Buffet Vert by Matisse. This subtle and sophisticated painting illustrates an anecdote in Chapter 11, which tells how an untutored mind was gradually won over to the contemporary style of painting, by being exposed to its charms each day. *Collection of Musée National D'Art Moderne, Paris. Ektachrome by Crea Color Photo Studio, Rome, and New York City.*

the students to simplify their treatment. It showed where the darkest shadow falls, where the half-tone creeps around and where the high-light and reflected light come.

My usual routine is to paint for two to two and a half hours, with occasional rests for the model, and then have at least a half hour's break for refreshment. It is good for the sitter to relax completely and for you to watch him during this period and notice how he changes when not posing. I usually work from ten till twelve-thirty and then have lunch with my sitter. Soon I am eager to get to work again. This is one of the most valuable moments of the day. You and the model are both refreshed, the paint is wet and your critical eye can at once see what developments are needed. I like a portrait to develop by a natural process of growth.

> You should now proceed from one part to another as each seems to demand attention. Spend some time on the clothes, scrubbing boldly over the canvas, relating your tones to the backgound, neck and face. If you are painting a white collar, notice how the white accent helps you to check your flesh tones.
>
> One of the most important factors governing the technique of oil painting is that what you leave on the canvas at the end of a sitting will vitally affect your next day's work. Hard edges and bad drawing cannot easily be got rid of once the painting is dry. As the sitting draws to a close, keep this in mind. You want to be able to paint freely over it next time. Simplify your shadows, merge your edges, avoid accidental or uninteresting forms in the hair and clothes. Check vital distances. If you feel there is too much paint on the canvas, it is a good trick to take a piece of newspaper and press it firmly against it for a few moments. Pull it off carefully and you will find it has done your work no harm and only removed superfluous paint that might otherwise be in your way later. A newspaper is better than scraping off with a palette knife, which sometimes leaves a slippery surface. The paper leaves a pleasant texture on which to paint later.

At the end of your first sitting the basis of the portrait should be on the canvas, full of suggestion for future development, basically sound in structure and composition.

9 Approach to Portrait Painting: II

When you start the second sitting, the first thing to do is to spend several minutes comparing what is on the canvas to the model. Your fresh eye is invaluable. Be severe with yourself. Painting a portrait needs self discipline. When I am working, I divide myself into two people, the free painter and the harsh teacher. It is no good being lenient, saying things will do when you know very well that they are not good enough. Stand back and decide whether there are any basic inaccuracies in the structure and plan to correct them as you proceed.

The plan for the second sitting (or third if you have spent one sitting on the pose and planning), is to develop the forms, intensify the color and study the individual characteristics of the sitter. It is still a time for holding back; in the next sitting you finally commit yourself to the whole truth.

What I enjoy about the second sitting is the fact that all the important initial decisions have been taken, about the pose, composition and so on, and the final ones are still to come. There is time to breathe. You have a pleasant foundation of color to build on, there is opportunity for study and experiment. You are not yet committed.

DEVELOPING FORM AND INTENSIFYING COLOR:

As always, begin by re-stating the background against the head. There is no need to re-paint it as if it were the bathroom wall. Look at the silhouette of the head and start at a place where the hair may have changed its form, thus tackling two problems at once. Proceed as before, working the background and hair together. Paint thinly, keep the hair simple and watch for any changes since the previous sitting, developing any forms you find more attractive. Do not be concerned with texture and sheen, it is only at the edges that you can suggest its softness. If you are painting a man, be sure you feel for the shape of the skull underneath. When you come to the area where the hair touches the face, particularly where it grows from the forehead, be sure that you keep the edges extremely soft, otherwise it may look like a wig. You may notice a cool grey-green area between the forehead and the hair which will help you separate the two by an intermediate tone.

Now start on the face. It is a good plan to begin at the top and come down slowly, strengthening the color and developing the form as you go. Here are some useful points to remember at this stage.

Keep your areas of light and shadow simple.

Keep the lights and half-tones cool and the cast shadows warmer.

Pure flesh color shows clearest between the highlights and the cool half-tones.

Do not overdo the modeling on the light side of the face. A highlight on the cheek or nose may give the impression that the surrounding tones are darker than in fact they are. It is more important to get the sense of the receding planes from the cheekbones to the jaw, than to search for small changes of form and color under the eyes and between the nose and mouth.

Treat the features simply. The eyes should be more definitely suggested, but not too much as yet.

Define the bone in the bridge of the nose. Watch the construction of the tip, where it turns under. Define the nostrils.

Keep the edge of the mouth soft and emphasize the shadow between the lips rather than the shape of the lips themselves.

Notice that the chin is an egg-like shape and that the jaw has a bone inside.

Feel for the cylindrical shape of the neck and notice how the shadow of the jaw helps you to define this.

REMEMBER THE EGG!

Above all, keep in mind that you are going to paint over this again and that the sitting is strictly one for research. Spend some time on the clothes, but do not commit yourself to accidental folds and details. There is a solidly constructed body underneath of which you must be constantly aware.

During this sitting you will have been watching the play of expression on the face, and become familiar with the variations of modeling round the eyes and mouth. Also where the major accents will fall, maybe at the side of the cheekbone, on the eyes or under the nose or mouth. These things can already be suggested, but by no means in full color or thick paint. Hold back all final judgments until the next sitting.

These instructions are bound to be general. The age and sex of your sitter make a great difference. An older man's head will be more strongly defined and more easily caught than a middle-aged woman's, which always presents special difficulties. Tact, not to speak of chivalry, is needed to bring out the best features and modify the less pleasing aspects, such as a sagging jawline or pouches under the eyes. Children have to be constantly amused and interested to keep them still. Each sitter has special characteristics and you must study them individually. For that reason it is good to have a general program, such as I am outlining, rather than attacking a portrait in a haphazard manner.

By the end of the second sitting everything should be solidly constructed, the relative values true, but still on the light side, and no hard edges or thick pigment to interfere with your freedom next time. At this point it is a good thing to take a mirror, turn your back to the sitter and look at both your painting and the model together in the looking-glass. The comparison will at once show you anything that is seriously amiss, especially in the drawing. Try to correct this while the paint is still wet. It is much easier to do this now than later.

Now we come to the important third sitting. After six to eight hours preparatory work you are ready to commit yourself. Your plan today is to concentrate entirely on the head, covering it and the background next to it with wet paint in about two hours, and then spending almost as long after the lunch break painting into the wet paint.

Warn your sitter that you may need him a longer time and that the success or failure of the portrait may depend on an extra ten minutes work.

First of all, if the paint has "sunk" since last time, brush on some retouching varnish. This brings out the true values and makes the surface more receptive. Start again with the background, this time giving it its full color value. Re-state the silhouette of the head and as soon as possible, merge the hair into it. Paint the hair broadly, giving the darks their full value, but still holding back detail and accents which you can place with more confidence later on in the sitting. Use more paint than before on your brush, and give each value its full strength. Continue with the forehead, merging it into the hair, loading on the paint in the lightest parts to give it brilliance. Now you are really painting. The more white you use, the richer your paint will be, but if the color is too pale the result will look "chalky." You should still hold back reserves for the last part of the sitting, but a far wider range of values will give the whole head a tremendous lift.

Continue to cover the rest of the face, strengthening the modeling, defining the features, until the whole head has a new layer of paint. Move from one area to another, never staying too long on any one point. Now you can take your time over the eyes and mouth, and they will make the portrait come to life for the first time. During the whole sitting you should be at a pitch of excitement and concentration as the portrait develops before you. After a couple of hours work, relax completely before you come to the most exciting period of all. Then, in critical frame of mind, move freely over the whole head, from the hair to the eyes to the shadow under the chin, relating one part exactly to another. Give the mouth its full color, accentuate the interesting reflections in the eyes, darken the pupils and the line of lashes, model the cheeks more carefully, decide where the highlights will come in the hair, strengthen the shadow under the nose—do all the things you have been wanting to do from the beginning—have a good time.

If your construction is sound, the restraint you have shown so far will be fully repaid. There is, however, a limit to what you can do at this point. It is wiser to re-state your big values, such as the background, the broad sense of light on the forehead, the shadow on the cheeks, than niggle with features too much. There is another sitting ahead, or more than one if necessary, when some of the finer points and surface detail can still be painted.

Now we come to the fourth sitting. It is a good plan to ignore the face for a while and concentrate entirely on the lower half of the picture. Until this is completed you cannot see clearly what is still needed to finish the face.

DETAIL AND FINISHING:

Brush on some retouching varnish where needed, and as usual, begin by painting the background, this time next to the arms and shoulders. Paint the clothes broadly and simply in full color against the background. Seize hold of the character of the forms where they reveal the structure of the body beneath, and do not get involved with accidental folds. During this time you will have been unable to resist glancing at the head and noticing various things that demand attention.

When the lower half of the picture has been painted in, you may decide to return to the head for a while and work on both together. From now on you are painting the picture as a whole. You can concentrate on subtleties of feature, modifications in the modeling, simplifications of light, delicate and varied edges, stronger accents where needed. Guard against niggling and losing simplicity. The danger now lies in looking for too much detail at the risk of losing the big, simple forms.

Return to the dress and complete the whole picture. If the dress has required a whole sitting, be sure that the wet paint merges saitsfactorily with the dry. If you are a beginner, it is probably best to wait for a final sitting before returning to the face. You should never feel too rushed, although when painting a portrait a certain pressure always seems to be present. Spend the fourth sitting on the accessories and come freshly to the fifth to make the final improvements as described above.

How can you tell for certain when the portrait is "finished"? A moment comes when you feel that you have approached as nearly as possible what you originally hoped to achieve. If this is expecting too much, then there also comes a time when, instead of the portrait getting better it begins to lose some of its freshness. If you go beyond this point, merely piling on more detail and pigment, you are likely to spoil everything. There is a limit to what you can successfully achieve in any one study, and if you go on too long the result will look lifeless and tired. You must stop as soon as you find this beginning to occur.

As you become more experienced, you will want to attempt larger portraits including the hands. Great care must be taken to pose your sitter naturally and let the hands fall in a characteristic manner. Paint each hand at one sitting, merging the edges into their surroundings where necessary, and pay particular attention to their structure, both at the knuckles and wrists.

A QUICK SKETCH IN ONE SITTING

I have described at some length how to paint a head and shoulders in four or five sittings. Should you feel inclined to have an attempt in one sitting, it can be great fun to let yourself go and see what happens. Before starting, it is a good idea to rub some warm grey all over the canvas, and then *wipe most of it off again,* leaving a moist, toned surface, not too oily or wet, but pleasantly receptive. A mixture of ivory black and burnt sienna dissolved in turpentine and copal oil medium spread on with a large brush will do very well. In three or four hours, see if you can make a rapid study, using the same principles and practice as before, but telescoping them all into one sitting. Draw in the head with a brush, using a darker grey than you rubbed on as a foundation, and then start as usual with the background and hair. This time, because the canvas is darker in tone, your light flesh color will show up immediately against it. The moist surface will keep you moving freely, but be sure that it is not too oily so that you find yourself slipping about. The longer you can hold back from painting the features in detail the better. Seize hold of the big forms and the structure as soon as possible, and place the features as accurately as you can. Keep moving over the surface, never staying long on one part. As one area develops, it will immediately show what is to be done in the part next to it. Work as rapidly and freely as possible, using fairly thick paint in the lighter parts almost from the beginning. You will find that the excitement will carry you along and perhaps your sketch will have a vitality that can be achieved no other way.

If you are dissatisfied with the result, take a piece of newspaper and remove the superfluous paint. You could then try to repaint it in one more sitting, using what is left of the first as a foundation.

THE INDIRECT METHOD

For a completely opposite approach, you can begin by painting the portrait in monochrome. A cool grey or green make an excellent foundation. Put out five gobs of white paint on your palette and add a minimum of ivory black or terra verte, a little more to each one until they are evenly gradated. The darkest one should still be a fairly light tone and the lightest pure white. Having drawn in your portrait, exactly as before, paint it entirely in monochrome for two or three sittings, building it up in stages until you have made a full record of form and structure. The tones must be in their true relationship, only much lighter in key. Your painting should be comparable to a piece of sculpture, only concerned with form and modeling. The light portions can be put on with fairly thick paint towards the end, to give a quality of richness to the foundation. You must wait for a considerable period before painting over it with color, because the thick paint may take as long as a week to dry.

The most difficult part comes when you begin to paint in color over the monochrome. You naturally wish to get rid of the grey as soon as possible, so that you can judge your color relationships clearly. As usual, start with the background and hair, keeping the paint transparent or semi-transparent by painting very thinly and using a certain amount of medium, so that the modeling shows through. At first you may be afraid of losing too much, but you will soon discover that if you keep your paint thin, the underpainting will show through clearly.

Do not attempt more than covering the monochrome with color at one sitting. Until this is satisfactorily achieved you cannot see the portrait as a whole. You may be a little confused when you cover the very light areas with flesh color and find the tone drops somewhat, but this is only a transitory effect until the monochrome is completely covered.

One danger of this method is that any faults in drawing in the monochrome will be very difficult to eradicate, so be sure that it is structurally sound before painting over it in color. If you have to make radical changes, you will have to paint more thickly on top to eliminate the mistake underneath.

A well painted, soundly constructed monochrome can be a very helpful foundation, but an unsatisfactory and inaccurate one will be a great handicap. During the final sittings you will paint much as in the direct method. Both methods are worth trying and it is a matter of personal taste which you prefer.

CHARCOAL PORTRAITS

Charcoal is a very expressive medium for drawing portraits. It is stronger and more effective than pencil, but there should be no smudging or rubbing otherwise the drawing will look sooty and dirty. I always use it on the point, previously sharpened by a razor blade. Charcoal is very useful when you are trying to catch subtle changes of expression. Its great merit is that it can be delicately removed with putty rubber without harming the drawing. It can be used for life-sized heads and reproduces well in print. Care must be taken not to smudge the drawing while at work, and it must be fixed immediately when it is finished with charcoal fixative, because it smears at the slightest touch. Do not go on too long and turn it into a full tone drawing. It should retain the character of a true drawing and only be concerned with form. There is no reason, however, why the darkness of the hair and of some of the deepest shadows should not be indicated, but do not let the result become photographic in tone values.

I have drawn upward of 1500 charcoal portraits and have found it the ideal medium when an effective and accurate likeness is required. I always begin a portrait at the bridge of the nose between the eyes, and work outwards from there. I establish the relationship between the eyes on either side of the nose as accurately as possible, and judge the length of the nose. I test this along the feature itself as well as by checking the distance between the inner corner of the eye and the wing of the nostril. This is always a much shorter distance than you imagine and is more easily judged than the whole length of the nose by itself. Then I work rapidly up the temple to the hair and down the cheek-bones to the mouth. Then comes the jaw and chin and the placing of the ear. I constantly return to the starting point at the bridge of the nose to check distances. The advantage of starting at the firm bone structure is that it never changes and is a central point from which to judge all distances. This is a far better method than "blocking in" the head as a whole, because the likeness depends so very much on the correct relationship between the eyes and nose, and it is safest to get this right to begin with and work outwards from there. Once the whole head has been drawn in, I move from one part to another, gradually developing the forms and features together, until it is finished. I keep the drawing as light as possible until near the end when I place the darks with great care.

Portrait painting is the most difficult and concentrated work I know. Do not be discouraged if it takes time before you paint a good head. The more confidence you have in your technique, the more you will be able to devote to the psychology of your sitter. You should get to know him, if possible, beforehand, so that you have a clear conception of the portrait before you start. However well you know your subject, you will gain more knowledge of him during the sittings. The whole portrait should evolve naturally. If the sitter is relaxed and at ease and you are in sympathy with one another, an emotional current should pass between you which affects every touch you put on canvas. There are times when you are bound to be more concerned with "expression" than others, but it cannot be superimposed on a lifeless head. The likeness and character must evolve from the very beginning along with the rest of the painting.

Becoming a good portrait painter needs years of study and is not to be embarked upon lightly. It is a difficult and demanding profession, but if it is your vocation and you have the talent, it is also one of the most rewarding.

10 Abstract and Non-Objective Painting

You must not have the mistaken idea that abstract painting is less "difficult" than representational. To do any kind of painting well is difficult. It may be harder to estimate the true merits of abstract painting, and it may be easier for an artist to cover his inexperience when his work is free from comparison with nature. But the serious painter who attempts to work in the non-objective manner is going to find plenty of tough problems to solve if he is to satisfy himself and others that he is doing good work.

I am convinced that there are permanent standards by which to judge all good painting, representational or not.

When you consider the thousands of *bad* pictures that have been painted, which are completely representational, it is obvious that an ability to copy nature accurately carries with it no assurance of doing work of artistic value. Given some native ability, any hard-working painter can, in time, become proficient in making a recognizable representation of what is before him. In fact, the purpose of this book is largely concerned in helping you to do just that! Serious artists have always had certain aims in common and non-objective painting contains many of the essential qualities of good painting of all periods.

During a recent visit to the Metropolitan Museum in New York, I was struck by the intense jewel-like beauty of a small Vermeer. The picture was called "Woman With a Jug." It hung in a row of excellent Dutch pictures and it was immediately clear that it out-classed them all. Although not more than a few inches square it seemed to contain the very essence of beauty. "Here," I thought, "if we can pin it down, we are very close to the heart of the matter. Within this small area is the secret of great painting." Looking through an archway into another gallery, I could see a large picture by a little known painter, Solimena, with many figures and a complex design. It was an elaborate composition and carried out with immense skill, apparently needing a great deal more knowledge than the picture of a single figure standing by a window. Yet I knew that the one was pretentious and second-rate and the other the work of a consummate artist. On pages IX and X of picture insert you can judge the pictures for yourself.

Let us see if we can penetrate a little further into the mystery of art by careful analysis of the qualities of the Vermeer. The subject was one he loved and understood, the quiet comfortable life of the Dutch burgher of the 17th century. Everything is rich in quality and in good taste. His world is snugly enclosed within four walls, the cool light from the stained glass window playing softly over everything within their safe enclosure. A woman with no specially outstanding features stands serenely before us, neither stiff nor consciously graceful. All is peace and contentment in her small world. This is Vermeer's subject, "domestic interior with figure."

Now let us examine the picture a little more deeply. It is not the subject which gives us the feeling of complete satisfaction, but the way in which it has been treated. Every object has been placed with a feeling for its exact relationship to the next. The picture has not only been composed in a beautiful, flat pattern, but is a solid composition in depth. Purely as a design, the various shapes are perfectly integrated both in line and color. The white of the collar sings out against the quiet background and rich dark blue dress. The accent of red on the tablecloth is the exact contrast needed against the various cool tones. The vertical edge of the map on the wall stabilizes the sloping lines of the figure which stands as a simple triangular shape below. The note of clear blue on the chair is surrounded by darker tones, and the light catches just enough of the shining pewter to give an accent exactly placed to balance the light on the collar.

The solid rectangular table stands in front of the cone-shaped figure and both are perfectly related to the wall and the window which are at right-angles to one another. The design is conceived in *depth* as well as on the surface of the picture and its rhythm and balance are almost mathematically worked out. All these qualities are *abstract* ones.

In addition to these we are also aware of the nature of the objects represented, but if they were not so well related to each other, or so beautifully harmonized in color and tone, the picture could just as well be any study of an interior. It is the *abstract* qualities which give the picture its greatness as a work of art and not its representational ones, exquisitely carried out as they may be. In addition the picture has a richness of paint, a thick creamy surface texture that can be fully appreciated only in the original.

I hope I have made it clear that, although the Vermeer is painted in a completely representational manner, the greatness of his work depends on the abstract qualities of his harmony, color and design. The fact that in this painting the figure has been treated in a very detached manner adds further point to the argument. Many great artists have been much concerned with humanity. Rembrandt, perhaps the greatest of all, identified himself completely with the problems of human beings. His position in the world of art is partly based on his intense psychological perception, his deep compassion and understanding of human nature. Nevertheless there are many fine artists who appear completely detached from humanity, whose reputations have been gained solely on their handling of aesthetic problems. Cezanne is an example of an artist who painted in this manner. However, Cezanne was still very close to nature and his pictures were all founded on direct experience.

Matisse was also chiefly concerned with aesthetic problems. On page XI of the picture insert I show a painting by him representing an "Interior at Nice." Above it we see a vast canvas by Paulo Veronese, "Christ Healing a Woman." I am not concerned here with how much Veronese was involved with religion and humanity. That he was a great painter was certain and that he could paint human beings with style and a sense of drama is unchallenged. The beauty of this picture, however, is very largely due to its color and composition. Notice the subtle harmony of cool greys, blues and golden browns, and how the accents of orange on the kneeling woman's cloak and the red on the drapery at the foot of Christ are perfectly placed. The sweeping diagonal from lower left-hand corner, from the woman's arm up to the head of Christ, is stabilized by the strong uprights of the pillars. The blue sky on the left is surrounded by color values that bring out its cool intensity. The perfection of intricate detail is merged into the bold over-all pattern. The brilliance of the silver dress, white sleeve of Christ's garment and woman's shoulder in the right-hand lower corner, form a triangle of balanced accents.

Now let us study the Matisse. Notice the similar strong diagonal, this time made by the curtain and steadied by the window. The blue of the sea is surrounded by colors that again bring out its cool intensity. The harmony of silver-grey and golden-brown is also emphasized by the orange colored pineapple and the red tablecloth. There is enough similarity in the two pictures to show that both Matisse and Veronese were interested in the same problems of color and composition. Veronese lived in a time when artists were commissioned to paint large pictures with religious themes, and no doubt he enjoyed creating elaborate figure compositions. Matisse was free to paint what he chose, and his room in Nice provided a starting point. The subject of the two paintings was very much the same—an abstract problem of color and form relationships.

It was Picasso and the Cubists who started to move away from natural forms. At first it was possible to detect the shapes of pierrots and guitars, bottles and fruit as motifs in their pictures. But gradually even these faded away and a new school of non-objective painting emerged. Color and form, rhythm and pattern, balance and line become the subject of the picture. Paint texture and richness of surface were also included.

Some abstract painters still use nature as a starting point; others are able to base their pictures on purely aesthetic experiences, entirely divorced from outside inspiration.

I recall a conversation at a party given by a collector of contemporary abstract paintings. Two or three guests were discussing a large picture. A woman turned to me and said in a rather aggrieved tone "I know I'm extremely ignorant and uneducated and know very little about painting, but I cannot understand in the least what the artist is trying to get at, or what the picture is supposed to represent. Can you?"

"Before I answer," I replied, "I would like to challenge your statement. I don't believe for one moment that you consider yourself ignorant or uneducated or that you think you know nothing about painting. I should imagine that you are quite knowledgeable and are merely irritated because you think the artist is trying to pull a fast one, and you don't like to feel imposed upon."

The lady had the grace to look a little contrite.

"You may be right," she said, "but seriously, what do you think of the picture. Can you explain what is good about it?"

"Do you like the color?" I asked.

"Oh, the color is very pleasing," she replied.

"Do you like the bold rhythms?"

"Yes, they are most agreeable."

"Does the overall pattern please you?"

"Certainly, but. . . ."

"Then what more do you want from a picture?"

"But what does it *mean*?"

"What does a fugue by Bach mean?"

"There's no more in the picture than that?"

"That is all, and in my opinion, more than enough," I said, and at last the lady seemed satisfied with my "explanation."

I have repeated this anecdote because I believe it represents the attitude of many people to abstract painting and may help to interpret the aims of the non-objective artist more clearly.

How then, should you, as a beginner, set about starting abstract painting. You must not be content merely to make meaningless combinations of color, slapping on the paint indiscriminately, (I believe some people have put up a case even for this approach!) I think you should begin by basing your picture on an experience derived from nature and then gradually, if you wish, move into a world of your own imagination. At first you will find complete freedom of expression a mixed blessing and you would be wise to create some laws of your own within the boundaries of your canvas. Uncontrolled freedom can only lead to confusion and chaos.

Abstract painting is by its nature so wide in scope that I can only make a few practical suggestions which may be useful.

1 Have a well defined purpose behind your picture. For instance, create a work that will please by balance and harmony or, by contrast, shock by violence and disharmony. There should be a definite intention which the onlooker may discover for himself. It may be to create something severely simple, like the work of Mondrian, who

achieved a calm and concentrated balance, or emotional and spontaneous like the painting of Kandinsky, full of flowing shapes and prismatic color.

2 If you are using recognizable motifs, be consistent within your own picture. Stick to the laws that you yourself lay down. If you distort natural objects in one portion, see that the distortion is reasonably equal throughout the picture.

3 You may attempt to interpret your emotion when confronted by a particular scene, and by rejecting all external and extraneous matter, concentrate entirely on the expression of your feelings.

4 You can base your design on a purely mathematical conception, either flat or solid as the case may be. It could, for instance, be founded on squares and circles and triangles, or cones, cubes or cylinders. There are harmonies based on scientific theories of color, orange with blue, yellow with violet, black with white.

5 You may wish to fill your picture with dream-like symbols, like Marc Chagall or the naive motifs by Paul Klee. Symbols figure largely in abstract painting and add interest to the picture by the associations suggested. If you study the work of the best abstract painters, you will discover that each is attempting to solve certain aesthetic problems.

I strongly advise all beginners to master the technique of painting from nature first. I feel certain this is essential, and however far you may later depart from natural forms, the experience will be invaluable.

11 Composition and Content

In the previous chapter I analyzed the composition of a Vermeer, Veronese and a Matisse. There is no better way to learn about composition than by studying the work of great painters of all periods. Underlying most works of art you will discover a firm architectural basis and a constant rhythmic flow of form and color. Make a point of studying good reproductions and see whether you can perceive these aspects, quite apart from what the pictures represent. Better still, study the original works whenever you get the opportunity. No reproduction gives the true color exactly or can more than suggest the beauty of the picture itself; but for the study of formal composition reproductions will serve well enough, and these are readily obtainable. In fact, more than ever before, the student has the whole range of the world's art to study at leisure.

From time to time, writers on art have attempted to formulate a set of rules of pictorial composition. Although each artist tends to make his own rules, certain fundamental ones still remain constant. I propose to analyze a few more of my favorite pictures to see if we can discover what some of these are.

Let us begin with Rembrandt's "Young Girl at an Open Half-Door," in the Chicago Art Institute, one of the loveliest pictures in the world. On the purely representational level it shows an appealing figure of a young woman, painted realistically, without any concession to prettiness. The mood is one of serenity, yet underneath you sense a warm, eager expectancy. A subtle smile suggests tenderness. The face is beautiful.

So much for the subject—now let us look at the composition. The color is a restrained harmony of cool blacks, warm browns and ochres, revealing the strongly lighted flesh tones, with the red necklace as the one brilliant color accent. The surface pattern is one of alternating light and shadow. The right arm is revealed in a clear dark silhouette, with the right hand remaining in shadow, the left arm is in shadow and the left hand clearly defined in silhouette. One side of the window is dark and the other light. The figure is solidly constructed—notice the egg-like head!—and stands firmly behind the window and some distance in front of the background. The whole picture is balanced, strong and satisfying on every level.

Now let us look at a modern Dutchman's work, the "Bedroom at Arles" by Van Gogh. Van Gogh had the power of investing the simplest objects with significance, through the intensity of his own vision.

On the face of it, this picture is a direct representation of a typical small room in Provence, containing a bed, a table and a couple of chairs. How did he manage to make this into a striking picture? Chiefly by selecting certain aspects, emphasizing them and rejecting others completely. He selected the characterisic shape, color and texture of each object and wove them into a harmony of brilliant color. Like Rembrandt and Vermeer, he carefully places a bright red accent, made by the blanket, and surrounds it with cool colors. Unlike the earlier masters, he has rejected contrasts of light and shadow—or chiaroscuro—and concentrated on the color pattern. He achieves recession by ingeniously emphasizing the perspective lines of planked floor and the bed, leading the eye to the window with its heavily stressed dark blue uprights and horizontals. We are not only inside Van Gogh's bedroom, but inside his private world of color, form and pattern.

Degas' approach to composition was different. He possessed exquisite and unfailing good taste. This is a rare gift of inestimable value. It is instinctive and inborn, or at least acquired at a very early age through environment. Many painters have lacked good taste, but made up for it with a compensating imagination and vitality.

Degas was also a superb draughtsman and colorist, but his compositions sometimes seem haphazard. He was intrigued by the new invention of the camera, not for its power to imitate nature, but its ability to catch the passing moment of action. He delighted in apparently accidental grouping and unorthodox but characteristic poses. He observed nature with an acute and sensitive eye. Using his unerring sense of fitness, he would rearrange his sketches, drawn from life, and base an unusual composition on them, placing them together daringly within the four sides of his canvas, even cutting across a figure when he thought necessary. Who but an original artist would have had the courage to place the two characters in the "Absinthe Drinkers" up in the top corner and fill the rest of the canvas with flat marble tables? Yet somehow we accept the composition as right. Would placing the figures one inch higher or lower have been "wrong"? In the pictures of Vermeer, Veronese and the great Renaissance masters, everything seems almost mathematically balanced; you get the feeling that their pictures are built on a series of immutable laws. With Degas, you sense more of the lucky accident, controlled by a brilliant and original mind. He knew instinctively, not only where to place his figures, but which areas to leave almost untouched and which to paint with great delicacy. He is a master of edges and emphasis, as well as of exact color relationships. Could Degas be "wrong"—could he make mistakes? Every master falls below his own standards on occasion. You can only judge a Degas picture by comparing it with another Degas, and as far as I am concerned, he is always completely satisfying. Every good artist creates laws of his own and those are the ones by which he must chiefly be judged. Painters as productive as Degas, Renoir or Picasso, being only human, have sometimes painted below their own highest level. In the final analysis we must search for qualities in paintings that are by universal agreement to be admired wherever they are in evidence. The word "beauty" is too subjective to be taken as an absolute standard. What may seem beautiful to the untrained eye may be mere superficial prettiness to the educated one, and what may appear positively ugly to one, may have real beauty for another. That beauty is in the eye of the beholder is never more true than when it comes to art.

We should look for such qualities as strength, simplicity, sensitiveness, delicacy, serenity, vitality, gaiety, harmony, balance, rhythm, imagination, variety, splendor, courage, sympathy, originality.

In the same way weakness, muddle, inconsistency, strain, artificiality, sentimentality, vulgarity, clumsiness, cheapness, awkwardness and emptiness are all to be deplored.

Some ideas such as distortion are controversial. If the distortion is consistent, imaginative, rhythmic and vital, such as in El Greco and Picasso, it adds greatly to the total effect.

One of the things we must be on guard against is the dislike and rejection of the unfamiliar. A story that illustrates this point occurred when I was in charge of a control tower on an airfield in Palestine during the last war.

It was necessary to have a cupboard and notice-board made, and these were painted a certain color green at my suggestion. Walking down the main street of Tel-Aviv, I chanced to see some reproductions of modern paintings in a shop window, among which was one by Matisse representing a cupboard exactly like mine, with some fruit and a cravat on top. I could not resist buying it and pinning it on the official notice board above the cupboard. When the young and rather officious Wing-Commander saw it there, he inquired crisply, "What the hell is that supposed to be?" I answered, "That, Sir, is a painting of my cupboard, done twenty years ago by Matisse." "It's terrible," he said, "it's all crooked and out of drawing—a child could have done better." "Matisse is considered one of the world's great artists," I replied. "Rubbish!" snapped the Wing-Commander and stamped out of the room.

The next day he was back, irresistibly drawn to the picture. "What's good about it anyway?" he asked, "Can you possibly explain to me?" I did my best, pointing out the charm of its color, the simplicity of its design, the overall pattern, the underlying strength of the composition. Still unconvinced, he returned to look at it each day. After about a month, he came to the control tower to greet a friend who had just flown in from Cairo. "By the way, old man," he said, "See that picture on the board? Jolly good isn't it—done by one of the world's greatest artists!"

It was not I who had finally won him over, but the picture itself. Gradually its charm had worked on him and the unfamiliar aspects had become pleasing instead of irritating. It is always wisest to approach unfamiliar work with a readiness to understand and enjoy rather than to make snap judgments. This does not mean that you have to like everything that is generally accepted as good. Everyone has the right to their personal taste, but this can be improved and its scope enlarged by a sympathetic approach and a readiness to understand what the artist is aiming at. It is easy to enjoy the flowing rhythms and joyous color of Renoir, but not so simple to grasp the strong, uncompromising grandeur of Cezanne, who may have lacked Renoir's facility. We can all appreciate Picasso's blue and pink periods, though not everyone can follow him through a lifetime of dynamic experiment with equal pleasure. Picasso has never ceased to explore, often using harsh and violent forms of expression. Yet his harlequins and circus folk are gently romantic in conception, and a poetic feeling runs through much of his work. Warmth and gaiety are present in many pictures of his classical period; horror and anger are magnificently portrayed in "Guernica."

The content of an artist's work reflects his personal reactions to life, his ideas about religion or society, the beauty or squalor of the world around him. A painter has something to communicate and chooses form and color as his means of expression. Only abstract and non-objective painting is remote from life and concerned solely with aesthetic emotions and the problems of picture making. For this reason I feel it can never take the place of painting that is immediately concerned with life, although it will continue to exist alongside and help to increase the scope of the painter's art.

My personal taste is for the artist who has a point of view about humanity, whether detached and penetrating like Degas, warm and tender like Renoir, or fierce and relentless like Goya. Rembrandt is the greatest of all in his understanding and compassion. I enjoy the healthy vigor of Franz Hals as well as the poetic delicacy of Peiro della Francesca.

If you are planning to be a professional artist, your years of study should be devoted to mastering your medium and gaining a technique that will express what you have to say. In fact your whole career should be a continuous development of greater freedom of expression.

Every artist has a right to choose his subject and express himself in his own way. His choice may sometimes be deplored, but no one can deny him the right to make it, except from the standpoint of personal taste. It was foolish of the critics to attack Manet for painting "Olympia" because she was a courtesan, or "Le Dejeuner sur L'Herbe" for showing a nude woman picnicking among a group of young men. They took up moral attitudes which have nothing to do with art, and blinded them to the beauty of the picture. An artist must be allowed full freedom of choice both for his subject and treatment. When he is specially commissioned, whether to paint a portrait or to carry out a particular theme, only the patron has the right to comment on whether the result is successful from his point of view. There is no end to the stories of angry patrons who have disapproved of the finished work, or of even more bitterly resentful artists who have scorned their patron's lack of taste and understanding. Rembrandt's "Nightwatch" offended the burghers whose faces were not clearly shown, Sir William Eden refused to accept Whistler's portrait of him, Lord Leverhulme cut up his picture by Augustus John, Sir Winston Churchill was unhappy about Graham Sutherland's interpretation. Michelangelo expressed the point of view of the artist when he retorted scornfully to a critical patron, "Who will care in a hundred years' time whether the picture is like you or not—it will live as a work of art!"

It would be an interesting piece of research to discover the relationship between an independent income and the quality of an artist's work. Many great painters, including Velasquez, Rubens and Van Dyck thrived on the patronage of the rich and powerful, and succeeded in producing great works of art which apparently satisfied both themselves and their patrons. Rembrandt rebelled against the drudgery of portrait painting and produced much of his greatest work in poverty, without an independent income but with independence of spirit.

Van Gogh survived only by grace of his brother's financial generosity, which allowed him to paint as he liked. Gauguin's genius survived hardship and financial pressure. Degas was wealthy, Cezanne had a small private income—so had Manet. Renoir achieved financial independence after twenty years of living from portrait painting.

It is the professional portrait painter whose work is the most uneven, when unsympathetic sitters as well as the pressure of time and money force him below his own standards. Reynolds, Gainsborough, Lawrence and Romney produced many inferior works for these reasons. Degas was in the happy position to refuse any commission he did not care to undertake, and his portraits are all fascinating.

Today, more than ever before, critics are ready to encourage new and original work, and a large section of the public is eager to understand what is being done. Dealers and collectors are prepared to help real talent, and the status of the artist is improving all the time.

Groups are also springing up everywhere for the gifted amateur, where work can be exhibited and interests shared with other enthusiasts.

In the following chapter I am going to break down and give a few hints how to cut corners, especially if you are painting as a pastime. I want to help you to enjoy yourself and paint the best pictures of which you are capable.

12 *Photographs:* HOW TO USE THEM OR MISUSE THEM

To write this chapter, I have had to conquer the Puritan that still remains in me. I learned to draw and paint the hard way, studying several months from the antique, and then for some years in the life class. The human body is composed of the most complex series of inter-related forms that exist, and therefore makes an ideal subject for study. The color of flesh is subtle, the tones delicate. In addition, the figure is such an important subject in art that it is invaluable to understand its construction thoroughly. Unless you have had an opportunity to work from life, it is unlikely you will paint a figure convincingly.

Having said this, I can, with a clear conscience, discuss the use of photographs. Photographs are now in general use by most artists. All "commercial" artists employ them continually and a great number of others who may not always wish to admit it. Sickert said that the camera was a good servant and a bad master, and I have found this to be the truth. The greater your knowledge of painting from life, the better use you will make of photographs. If your knowledge is small, and your skill insufficient, the results of using photographs will be deplorable. My advice is first of all to learn to paint the way I have outlined in the previous chapters. Then there is no doubt a camera can be an invaluable aid if used with intelligence and discretion.

There are many different ways it can be employed:

1 A landscape can be photographed at the same time that you make your color sketch and used instead, or as well as, a drawing.

2 If there is no time or opportunity to make a color sketch, you can photograph a landscape and make written notes of the color values.

3 You can even go so far (or sink so low) as to take a color photograph, have a slide made of it, project it on a screen and imagine you are on the spot!

4 You can use a photograph as a starting point for a composition. The camera can capture scenes of action which no artist could hope to record quickly enough. Public ceremonies, processions, sporting events, crowds, animals in motion and so on.

5 Commercial artists today employ professional models and photograph them in the particular scene or action they wish to illustrate. This helps to give their work the high standard of realism now required. Where formerly an illustrator would make many sketches from life, he can now save time and effort by using specially posed photographs instead.

6 Portrait painters often use photographs either to save sitters time or their own. In the case of posthumous portraits, there is no alternative, but many portrait painters use them even when the sitter is available, especially to help with clothes and accessories.

If you start to copy photographs before you have studied the real problems of color and form, you will not get very far. If you imitate flat tones and shapes without a real understanding of their nature, the results will be horrible. I've seen many such efforts that filled me with despair. To copy the surface of a photograph without grasping the truth underneath is a waste of time. The fact that you may achieve some resemblance to the photograph is completely misleading. The work is without value either as an exercise or a finished product. To use a photograph well, you must have learned how to paint first, then you will be able to "read" a photograph correctly and re-create the scene or objects it records. The camera has no power of selection and you must learn to reject all useless detail or accidental shadows. If a photograph has been retouched, you must realize what is missing and use your own judgment about what should have been taken out. You must notice whether a photograph distorts and makes the objects near the camera out of proportion. Some portrait photographs have harsh shadows and highlights—the inevitable trademark of the commercial photographer—and are quite unsuitable for a painter to use.

Here are some good ways to make use of photography. You may be a portrait painter with a client who is unable to give you more than one or two sittings, a fidgety child or a very busy man. Pose him in the studio in exactly the same light and position as if you were going to paint the portrait entirely from life. If you are sufficiently experienced as a photographer by all means take the pictures yourself, otherwise it is better to employ a professional. The negative must be big enough to allow the head to be enlarged to life size. Take as many photographs as possible, certainly not less than six, for people tend to become self-conscious in front of a camera and it is most important to catch a characteristic expression and a relaxed pose. The negative and prints should remain completely unretouched. Study the prints carefully and select the one with the most natural expression. Should the pose not be sufficiently relaxed, you may make use of an alternative print, but great care is needed to combine two photographs satisfactorily.

Have the head enlarged to life size on a glossy print about 10 inches x 12 inches. Usually a child's head is about 7½ inches, a woman's 8½ inches, and a man's 9 inches to 9½ inches. The whole photograph may need enlarging, but not necessarily to life size, so that you can see detail without strain.

You must work out by a simple mathematical process the proportion of the head in the original photograph to the area to be used in the painting. Suppose the head in the photograph is 3 inches long from the crown of the head to the chin, and when enlarged is 9 inches, a proportionate enlargement of 3 to 1. If your canvas is to be 24 inches x 18 inches the area of the photograph used will be 8 inches x 6 inches. You can cut out a rectangle of 8 inches x 6 inches from a piece of paper or cardboard and move the open framework over the photograph so as to find the best composition. Mark these boundaries with pencil on the photograph and measure exactly where the head will come in relation to the top and the sides. Using scotch tape, stick the enlargement of the head carefully in the exact relative position on the canvas, first placing a piece of graphite or carbon paper between it and the canvas. Stick them very firmly on four sides with scotch tape so that they absolutely immovable.

Take a pencil with a sharp point and very carefully press it along the outline of the essential features. Begin with the eyes and eyebrows, taking care that the iris, pupils and lids are very accurately traced. Then trace the nostrils and the wings of the nose, lips, hairline, shape of face and general shape of head. These are really all that are needed. No suggestion of form, shadows, tones or details of hair should be made. This, for once, is pure outline and a bare map. Indicate where the neck and ears come as well as the beginning of the shoulders or any portion of the dress. When this operation is complete, remove the photograph and tape which come off quite easily, and you should see a clearly defined outline on the canvas. Now draw the rest of the body in charcoal using, if you prefer, the process of squaring-up. Pin the enlargement onto the side of the canvas, as well as the original photograph, and using the usual mixture of thin, pale grey paint, model the head with your brush. You may first of all take a sable brush and very delicately strengthen the outline of iris and pupil and a few of the harder edges of the face. Do *not* repaint all the outlines which are merely guides, but paint freely over them. The great advantage of your tracing is that it is immovable and accurate and can be detected until the head is completely covered. This helps you to keep your drawing true and at the same time allows freedom of handling on top.

You now have the choice of painting the head entirely in monochrome, using white paint for the highlights and greys for the shadows, or you can keep the modeling and main features lightly drawn with a brush, leaving most of the canvas bare. If you paint a complete monochrome, do not make your tones as dark as in the photograph, but keep your range pale. Paint the whole picture, background and all in relatively light tones.

One great advantage of painting from a photograph is that you do not have to limit yourself to a three hour session but can work for a far longer time into the wet paint. The method I use myself is as follows: I draw in the whole picture accurately but lightly with a brush in pale grey. This does not take me more than an hour or two. Then I leave it to dry so that it remains a firm and useful guide all through the next day's work. On the second session I paint thinly over the whole picture in color to get rid of the white canvas, beginning as usual with the background round the head, keeping the treatment simple and light in key. The third day, I paint the head and its immediate background only, in full color and tone until it is all but finished, sometimes working for six or seven hours at a stretch. It is well worth the effort to keep a feeling of unity. Then I complete the rest of the canvas and only add a few essential accents or modifications to the face.

There is no reason to hurry, for the photograph never changes, but you should be careful not to over-work and make your painting too tight. Stand back quite often and compare what you have done to the photograph at the side of the canvas. Your enlargement is useful for seeing every detail, but the values of the smaller photograph are truer and therefore a better guide to follow most of the time. Should your sitter be able to come again, hold back some of the local color in the eyes, cheeks and hair. You will find it very exciting when he arrives to compare what you have done with the original. After the first shock, try to seize on the main differences that strike you immediately. Quite possibly you will have over-done some of the modeling which the camera has exaggerated and which the eye sees more simply. The portrait will probably need a process of simplification and strengthening of color but you will find the accurate foundation extremely helpful. Watch the face in movement and try to add liveliness to the expression. In a couple of hours you may be able to change a comparatively lifeless copy into a vital character study. If you have been working from a good color photograph—I don't mean "hand-tinted" which is useless—naturally you can paint with much more conviction than from a black and white one. If you are to have a sitting from life it is better to rely on this for the final color than on the photograph.

To paint a portrait from a photograph already taken and possibly without seeing the sitter, presents a different problem. In the previous case, the photograph, although of great importance, was used to help you paint from life and as an aid to memory. When you use a photograph taken previously, you may not have the opportunity of seeing the sitter at all, as in the case of a posthumous portrait; then your only guide is the photograph and your memory of painting other people from life.

> As before, an enlargement must be made and traced on to the canvas. You will find that if the enlargement is done from the print, instead of from a negative, it will be rather blurred and darker. It should only be used for the tracing and not as a guide to tone values for which you must only refer to the original photograph. The quality of photographs varies enormously, from amateur snapshots to professional "studio" portraits. If the expression and pose are not completely satisfactory, there is little chance that you can "improve" upon them in your painting. Sometimes a lucky snapshot will be more characteristic than a retouched professional photograph with hard shadows and artificial lighting.
>
> There are two color problems to solve. The local color, that is to say the coloring of the eyes, hair, and complexion, and the color values, the relationships as chosen by your own knowledge and taste. It is wisest to keep these values restrained in color to avoid making a wrong guess. The more information you can gather about the subject's appearance the better, and someone who knew them can help you enormously. You must search for the basic structure of the head and distinguish between meaningless shadows and tones and the essential modeling. Keep your half-tones cool and your cast shadows warmer. Rely on your knowledge of what *must* be there, even if it is difficult to see clearly. If your modeling is subtle, your structure sound, and the flesh tones appropriately warm and cool, the results should be perfectly satisfactory. If the subject is available, it is most useful to study him before you begin, but make no attempt to repaint your picture afterwards under lighting conditions which must inevitably be entirely different. The most you can do is to modify local coloring. It would be useless to try to "improve" on what you have done beyond this.

Sickert himself used photographs as a basis for many of his later paintings. Sometimes he chose one from an illustrated paper that struck his fancy because of its unusual composition or lively action. Early Victorian daguerreotypes made an appeal to him because of their old-fashioned charm and amusing costume. Being a fine artist, an excellent colorist and a man of wit and intelligence, Sickert was able to bring these qualities to whatever he painted. When he used a photograph as a starting point, he did not slavishly imitate, but extracted from them just what he needed, to make a work of art. There is no reason why you should not do the same within the limits of your particular capacity. If you see a photograph that appeals to you in a magazine or newspaper, use it as a basis for a picture. There is no need to copy this as carefully as if you were painting a portrait. Be sure that what appealed to you is transposed to your picture. It may be a strong silhouette, a lighting effect, the action or the dramatic values. Keep in mind that no picture is good unless the basic aesthetic qualities have been successfully tackled—color, form, rhythm, balance and so on. Without doubt photographs do help you to cut a few corners. As long as they are used intelligently, I can see no valid objection to employing them. Only when they are copied without knowledge, taste, selection or interpretive skill are the results to be deplored.

13 A Last Word

Not long ago I visited an exhibition in London called "A Century of Bad Taste." It was a chastening and thought-provoking experience. On view were paintings and other works of art, enormously popular in their day. Pictures that had been admired, won awards and been widely reproduced, now looked vulgar, sentimental and dull. From our lofty eminence we could afford to smile ironically at the poor taste of our predecessors. But could we? Could we be so sure of our own taste, our own absolute standards of judgments? Certainly we could now understand and appreciate the great French painters who were being derided when some of the atrocities of this exhibition were fetching high prices. But could we be so sure that some of the contemporary work on which so much praise was being showered would withstand the test of time?

To understand and fully enjoy good painting requires much knowledge, and even then, taste is fallible. When you learn to paint yourself, you begin to realize how much more there is to painting than you had ever suspected. Very few laymen get much beyond appreciating the subject matter of a picture, even if they remark that the color or design pleases or displeases them. One of the great advantages to be gained by learning to paint is the added pleasure you derive from looking at and appreciating the work of others.

Once you have learned the rudiments of painting, the important thing is to find your own form of self-expresison. In the last resort you must be your own master. You can learn from teachers, the work of others and, I hope, from a book like this. Then the time will come when you must sink or swim on your own.

One danger to beware of is the advice and opinions of others: of friends, relations and well-wishers. An artist's work invites criticism and comment. We are sensitive people, sometimes too ready to accept the opinions of those quite unqualified to give them. You must be neither too discouraged by adverse comment by self-appointed critics, nor too lifted up by praise from those whose good will is greater than their knowledge. You should have a purpose and know in which direction you are going. As you progress, you will discover the limits of your ability. If you have something to say, it does not matter if your talent is great or small as long as you learn to express it to the full. Augustus John, one of the greatest living artists, is a magnificent portrait painter and a masterly draughtsman. His sister, Gwen John, painted small delicate pictures, quiet in color, subdued in tone, quite unlike those of her famous brother. Most of them were of sensitive but homely girls placed against a simple background. By understanding the limitations of her gifts and not striving beyond them, she succeeded perfectly in expressing exactly what she wanted to say. In her own way she was just as fine an artist as her more famous brother.

When we were discussing Degas, I raised the question, could he be "wrong"? Once a painter has mastered his craft, his merits must be a matter of opinion and cannot be assessed as "right" or "wrong." As we have seen, opinion and taste vary enormously, and only time is the final judge. Meanwhile we must be true to ourselves and keep the small flame that we may have inside us burning steadily.

If you are young and setting out on a career, then try to become master of your craft, so that you can express yourself with complete freedom.

Should you be taking up painting as a pastime, give it the respect it deserves by taking it seriously. In this way you will derive the most pleasure and benefit.